6/15   3c   12/16

The Culinary Lives of
John & Abigail Adams
A COOKBOOK

Abigail Adams

John Adams

ROSANA Y. WAN

Schiffer Publishing Ltd

4880 Lower Valley Road • Atglen, PA 19310

Designed by Justin Watkinson Cover John Cheek
Type set in Amercian Scribe/True Golden™/Adobe Caslon Pro

ISBN: 978-0-7643-4669-9
Printed in China

Published by Schiffer Publishing, Ltd.
4880 Lower Valley Road
Atglen, PA 19310
Phone: (610) 593-1777; Fax: (610) 593-2002
E-mail: Info@schifferbooks.com

For our complete selection of fine books on this and related subjects, please visit our website at www.schifferbooks.com. You may also write for a free catalog.

This book may be purchased from the publisher. Please try your bookstore first.

We are always looking for people to write books on new and related subjects. If you have an idea for a book, please contact us at proposals@schifferbooks.com.

Schiffer Publishing's titles are available at special discounts for bulk purchases for sales promotions or premiums. Special editions, including personalized covers, corporate imprints, and excerpts can be created in large quantities for special needs. For more information, contact the publisher.

TITLE PAGE LEFT: Stuart, Gilbert. "Abigail Smith Adams (Mrs. John Adams)," oil on canvas. 1800/1815, overall: 73.4 x 59.7 cm (28 7/8 x 23 1/2 in.), *Courtesy National Gallery of Art, Washington. Signature courtesy Massachusetts Archives.*

TITLE PAGE RIGHT: Stuart, Gilbert. "John Adams," oil on canvas. c. 1800/1815, overall: 73.7 x 61 cm (29 x 24 in.), *Courtesy National Gallery of Art, Washington. Signature courtesy Massachusetts Archives.*

Dick Wray. *Photo courtesy Peter Brown*

In memory of Frank Merrill Dyer,
Dick Wray, and Marc Levine

"A Collection of her Letters for the forty five years that We have been married would be worth ten times more than Madame Sevigne's though not as perfectly measured in Syllables and Letters: and would or at least ought to put to the blus Lady Mary Wortley Montague and all her Admirers….So much! I say for simple Justice to Merit."

—*John Adams, referring to Abigail's letters to him, in correspondence to Mr. Van Der Kemp. Quincy, December 15, 1809*

"A good dinner is one of the greatest enjoyments of human life."

—*Kitchiner, William*, Apicius Redivivus:

"My Good Man is so very fat that I am lean as a rail."

—*Abigail Adams to Mary Smith Cranch, October 6, 1766*

"I endeavor to live in the most frugal manner possible, but I am many times distressed…"

—*Abigail to John Adams, July 16, 1775*

"It is My Destiny to Dig Treasures with My Own Fingers."

—*John Adams*

Contents

Acknowledgments

There are many people to thank for their help in making this book a reality. I didn't value the important roles that museums and libraries play when I was a child, and I'd like to thank my mother for taking me to my first museum, library, and first archeological workshop.

Growing up in Hong Kong and later in Houston, Texas, there were two things that I often took for granted: the history of the cities I lived in and food. Buildings were frequently demolished and rebuilt into multi-million-dollar skyscrapers. Food was so abundant that it seemed commonplace. There wasn't a sense of simplicity. On a trip to Colonial Williamsburg during eighth grade, I had my first cheesecake at Raleigh Tavern's bakery. This was the moment where I began my journey toward learning about the history of food and about the founding of this young nation, which I adopted as my own.

My love for reading history had started earlier, when I was in the fourth grade, but I had had a different focus. I had picked up an old copy of the *Oxford Junior Companion to Music* by Percy Scholes and become obsessed with the stories about the composers' lives. I had thought I might steer a similar course for myself.

But that dream changed when I read David McCullough's *John Adams* during my first semester in college. This book inspired me to become a historian, but it did more than that: learning about Adams made me want to become a better individual myself, to stand firm in my beliefs and values, to be curious, to not be afraid of asking questions, to think and write freely, and to voice my opinions. Like Adams, I want to dare to dream for a better future for others.

With this book, I bring together my early interests in food with my admiration for Adams and our founding fathers. My intention is to celebrate the lives of John and Abigail Adams by looking at their culinary history.

I dedicate this book to three men: my mentor, Frank Dyer, and my two best friends, Dick Wray and Marc Levine. Frank introduced

me to all kinds of foods that make America unique. Dick taught me to appreciate other ethnic cuisines and to make food with love. My dear friend, Marc Levine, simply taught me to eat healthfully and in moderation, while filling me in on the history of the Beatles and John Lennon. Like Dick, Marc taught me to appreciate home-cooked meals made with organic products.

In the years I have spent working on this book, I have trained myself to face culinary challenges (i.e. prepare a roast turkey), but I have also found myself on a life-changing journey. I am indebted to a growing list of people whom I have met along the way and who have helped shape this project by providing ideas, moral support, and contributions. This book project also helped me to continue my graduate work in scholarly research and historical writing, and gave me a platform to spread my love of history.

Nearly five years ago, I came to Boston in search of a strong history program to finish my undergraduate work. I met and befriended Gerard "Gerry" F. Burke, Sr., at Adams National Historical Park. Gerry owns Doyle's Café in Jamaica Plain and is a historian. Gerry helped me learn the history of Boston through the images displayed on the walls at his beloved tavern and thanks to his encyclopedic memories of people including John F. Kennedy, former Boston Mayor John F. Collins, Ted Williams, and John L. Sullivan, the boxer. It was also at Gerry's restaurant that we had a luncheon with two of his fellow historians, Jim Vrabal and Neil Savage. Gerry also strongly encouraged me to meet William M. Fowler, Jr., of Northeastern University, who led me to Professor Robert J. Allison at Suffolk University. Long after my graduation from college, Gerry continued to provide wisdom by reminding me to "keep punching" and make the best of my journey. Like my old friend, Frank, Gerry often advised me that "nothing is impossible." Gerry also said, "When you wake up every morning, you look at yourself in the mirror and say to yourself, 'I am the best God-damn person in the world,'" advice given to him as a young man by his old neighbor, John F. Collins, the former Boston mayor who suffered from polio.

Gerry's sense of humor and love of history always motivated me to follow my dreams. His advice on life encouraged me to continue to write and research history. I am deeply indebted to his endless support in my first book about the powerful couple that lived in Quincy, where we met.

I also met Tom Patterson that summer. He has provided much support for me in writing this book. I always enjoy listening to his stories.

I am indebted to two new friends for some of the photos in this book. Ed Nute took the photos of the food, and Patricia Bridgman is the reenactor dressed as Abigail Adams. These pictures show their talent and their love of history. I thank Pat for her stunning portrayal of Abigail and for her kindness. I thank Ed for his work and also for sharing stories of our love for Julia Child and our encounters with many amazing people, such as the world-renowned cellist Yo-Yo Ma.

I want to thank Professor William M. Fowler, Jr. for his patience, kindness, generosity, and moral support. His wisdom encouraged me to finish the book.

OTHERS TO THANK:

Caroline Keinath, Kelly Cobble, and the staff at the Adams National Historical Park. Michael Comeau and Jennifer Fauxsmith of the Massachusetts Archives. Jaclyn Penny of American Antiquarian Society in Worcester, Massachusetts. Mary Robinson of the Dorothy Quincy homestead in Quincy, Massachusetts.

Marianne Martin and Doug Mayo of the Rockefeller Library at the Colonial Williamsburg Foundation. Without their generous support and contribution, this book would not be possible.

Robert Wray, for his words of support. He has given his blessings for me to dedicate this book to his father, Dick Wray, from whom he inherited his sense of humor. Robert and I would joke that if I talked about John Adams once more, it would annoy his father.

Peter Brown, a photographer and a good friend of Dick, who was more than honored to give me a copy of our favorite picture of our beloved mutual friend.

The folks at Kerr High School in Houston, Texas, including Mr. Steve Levine, my U.S. government teacher, who gave me his blessings to dedicate this book to his son, Marc.

I thank the staff at the Massachusetts Historical Society for their dedication to educating the public and preserving American history. Their generosity in helping historians and researchers, such as myself, is worth more than I can say with these simple words. Their rich collection of the Adams family letters provides the core of this cookbook. Let us hope these letters will be remembered and preserved for future generations. They include valuable lessons about timeless matters such as hope, sacrifice, courage, and selfless service.

Especially I want to thank Mary T. Claffey, Anna J. Clutterbuck-Cook, Betsy Boyle, and Sara Georgini, editorial assistant for the Adams Papers. Sara has given me tremendous help in locating letters and transcribing some of them for the cookbook. She showed me how to use the online search engine for the Adams Papers Digital Edition. I thank Mary for her assistance in transcribing some Latin phrases in one of John Adams's letters. As for Betsy and Anna, they often gave me a warm welcome to the research facility.

Thank you also to my dear friends Pat Sebastian and Jan Briggs who constantly kept me positive throughout the project. I am thankful to have them by my side communicating in the old-fashioned way like John and Abigail Adams.

Thanks to the people at University of Houston-Downtown, such as Dr. Sara Farris and Dr. Merrilee Cunningham of the English department, who always look out for their students, including myself, helping them to succeed in their journeys and achieve their dreams.

As a sergeant in the Army National Guard, I'd like to thank my military family for constantly providing a moral compass, including my friend, Captain James Hairston, who is a chaplain at my former unit. His constant compassion and wisdom always motivated me to continue to fulfill the dream. I thank Elaine Heffernan for giving me moral support to stay positive during the editing process of the book.

I thank Beth Collins Wray. Her support and wisdom helped me as a writer and helped me follow my dreams. This book is dedicated in part to her husband, and I am honored to call her a friend.

Thanks to the folks at Suffolk University, including Coach Jim Nelson, Erica Lewis-Bowens, Judith L. Reynolds, Terry Bishop, Judith Entin, and many others who came in and out of my life and provided moral support.

And thank you also to the entire history department at Suffolk University, especially to Professor Bob Bellinger, whose input on historical interpretation, passion for history and food culture, and love of life made this project possible. One thing I learned from him is that historians are like explorers.

Thank you to my dear friend Professor Patricia A. Reeve for her countless contributions, unconditional encouragement, and support since the day I began this long journey. She gave me a fundamental lesson in conducting historical research when I was a student in one of her classes, History of American Medicine, Disease, & Healing. She contributed many hours of assistance to help me to write this book. Throughout the process of putting the work together, she raised many questions that helped the revisions. Her numerous suggestions and advice helped make this a better book. Her wisdom and compassion continues to inspire me.

Lastly, I want to thank the person who I met at the end of that fateful summer trip to Boston: the chair of the history department and my former undergraduate advisor at Suffolk University, Professor Robert J. Allison. I am indebted for his support when I first told him about this project in 2011, and later for his introduction to Eliza Parrish, former director of Suffolk alumni engagement, who I worked with to design an eighteenth-century lunch menu for the first collaborative history/alumni event at Old Sturbridge Village in Sturbridge, Massachusetts. It was one of my proudest achievements in this journey. In some ways, his books paved the road for the layout of this cookbook. His enthusiasm, wisdom, and endless support inspire many young aspiring historians/scholars including myself. His books helped me to write the timeline of John Adams's life and other historical events for this book, including the Boston Massacre, the Boston Tea Party, and the Siege of Boston.

About a month before I began this cookbook project, I baked a few things for pleasure from Walter Staib's *The City Tavern Cookbook* for the history department. He tried a slice of the Sally Lunn's cake and secretly took the rest of it home to his wife, Phyllis. She often praised my cooking, even though my skills are nowhere near Julia Child's or someone from Le Cordon Bleu. She asked detailed questions on how the process worked and what I put in that cake. Those conversations with Phyllis and Professor Allison made me realize something, which brought me back to what my old friend, Frank Dyer, tried to tell me many years ago: Incorporate the love of American history and cuisine together, and share that love with everyone. Because this is how humans survive as a civilization.

In some ways, these memories and simple words of thanks reflect the heart of this cookbook. Good food is not about making fancy and sophisticated dishes to impress one's family. It's not about spending lots of money for meals in fancy restaurants. It is simply about enjoying meals with the people one values the most—a spouse, family, or friends. Sharing good food is also a way to keep good company, as John and Abigail would dream about in their frequent separations through the fifty-four years of their marriage. By reading their letters, we come to appreciate life, family, friends, and also the history and culture of food.

Rosana Y. Wan

Photo by Ed Nute

Introduction

On November 29, 1798, Abigail Adams wrote to her husband, John, from their home in Massachusetts, about a day of thanksgiving.

> When I look Back upon the Year Past, I perceived many, very many causes for thanksgiving, both of a publick and private nature. I hope my Heart is not ungratefull, tho sad; it is usually a day of festivity when the Social Family circle meet together tho separated the rest of the year. No Husband dignifies my Board, no Children add gladness to it, no Smiling Grandchildren Eyes to sparkle for the plumb pudding, or feast upon the mind Eye. Solitary and alone I behold the day after a sleepless night, without a joyous feeling.[1]

In many letters, like this one, she displayed her dedication to her "untitled Man to whom I gave my Heart."[2] He too would write about wishing they could be together. "Your Solicitudes would be less if you were here. The Variety here would amuse you, and the Spirits of the gay enliven you, the Reasoning of the Wise assure you."[3]

Frequently separated due to John's career, the couple exchanged more than one thousand letters in their lifetimes. These examples are just a few that showcase their fifty-four years of marriage as "dearest friends."

They would fill their writings with details of their days, whether they were at home on their family farm in Massachusetts or traveling. Like her husband, Abigail had strong opinions. She once wrote to John, "my pen is always freer than my tongue."[4]

Although Abigail frequently suffered from poor health, she was in many ways ahead of her time. She used writing as her voice. She read a great deal as a child, taking advantage of her minister father's extensive library.

When John first met Abigail (nicknamed Nabby) Smith in 1759, he was not impressed with her: "Polly and Nabby are wits…P[arson] S[mith] Girls have not this fondness, nor this Tenderness… Fondling and Indulgence. They are the faulty Effects of good Nature…" he complained privately in his diary.[5]

But his opinion of her changed when they became reacquainted a few years later, as they shared their love for books and knowledge. Their shared sense of curiosity about the world drew the couple together, and they spent endless hours discussing books and ideas. In 1764, they were married. At age twenty-nine, John had met his match.

There were many times in their correspondence when they shared information about the types of food they ate during their numerous separations. They also wrote about food in letters to family members and friends. John Adams also recorded much about food and cuisine in his diary.

These letters and diary entries and their references to food are the basis for this cookbook.

Because their home was in Massachusetts, many of the recipes in this book are based on New England cuisine of that time period. However, the Adamses traveled a great deal, too. Because of John's work as a politician, diplomat, and statesman, they travelled up and down the East Coast and to Europe, dining both in big cities and in country homes.

For example, when John traveled with their sons Charles and John Quincy to pursue diplomatic matters in Paris, he wrote back to Abigail about French culture, including the cuisine. The Adamses first took up residence at Passy, along with Benjamin Franklin. Passy is now part of the 16th arrondissement of Paris, but in Adams's time, it was independent from the city. The Adamses later moved to a second residence in Auteuil, less than a mile outside Passy.

Most of John's letters from France are filled with criticisms of the French lifestyle and behavior, because they were so foreign to him. However, John actually harbored a secret love for the French. His letter from Passy of February 13, 1779 to his "dearest friend" back home reveals this love/hate relationship:

> I never had so much Trouble in my Life, as here, yet I grow fat. The Climate and soil agree with me—so do the Cookery and even the Manners of the People, of those of them at least that I converse with, Churlish Republican, as some of you, on your side the Water call me. The English have got at me in their News Papers. They make fine Work of me—fanatic—Bigot—perfect Cypher—not one Word of the Language—aukward Figure—uncouth dress—no Address—No Character—cunning hard headed Attorney. But the falsest of it all is, that I am disgusted with the Parisians—Whereas I declare I admire the Parisians prodigiously. They are the happiest People in the World, I believe, and have the best Disposition to make others so.[6]

John and Abigail's recorded culinary experiences, domestic and abroad, are all part of this cookbook.

Colonial cuisine and culture

Some dishes popular during the eighteenth century dated back as far as the Middle Ages, such as mince pie and boiled beef with cabbage. The English settlers naturally brought their own ideas of cuisine with them to the New World, including beef, chicken, stews, and breads. But that diet slowly changed in New England. By the mid-eighteenth century, traditional fare was augmented by foods that were seasonal and indigenous, such as corn and pumpkin. With the promixity to the ocean, seafood, including lobster, became a part of the daily diet. Because of the colder climate, New Englanders had difficulty growing other types of crops that were popular in the Southern or Middle Colonies, and so a distinct regional cuisine was developed.

Most recipes at this time were passed down from one generation to another orally. Sometimes a family member would record recipes on scraps of paper and bind them into a book to pass along to the next generation. But family recipes can be like family secrets. Though Abigail Adams was a prolific writer and may have written instructions on cooking for future generations, there is no historical evidence of this. She might have taught her only daughter, Nabby, to learn recipes through repetition. Later in life, Abigail had hired hands (free blacks) to help her with the cooking. They might have adapted her oral instructions on food preparation and cooking.

Cooking was manual labor in the Adamses' time. Foods were cooked on open fires. There were, of course, no modern stove or ovens. Cooking utensils resembled those used in Europe, including kettles and long metal spoons. Simple mechanical cookware was starting to appear in kitchens, such as clock-jack spits (roasting jacks) and reflector ovens.

The eighteenth century is regarded by many historians as the beginning of the Modern Period, and the making of some products—such as hard cider, cheese, and even butter—had become industrialized. These items were available for purchase. But Abigail Adams liked to make her own butter. She once wrote that she preferred to be a dairy woman.

Food served as a comfort for the colonists. It helped keep them warm during winter, and families united for meals. Abigail wrote in a letter from home to John Adams on May 7, 1783, of her wish to be dining with the man she loved:

> "…can you dine upon such a Slender number of dishes after having been accustomed to 50 and a hundred. Aya but say you true Friendship, tender affection and mutual Love are to be found there, and that is a feast I meet not with abroad. Come then and join in the Feast of reason and flow of Soul. Come and give happiness to her who know not either solid pleasure or real felicity seperated from you—and who subscribes most tenderly and affectionately."[7]

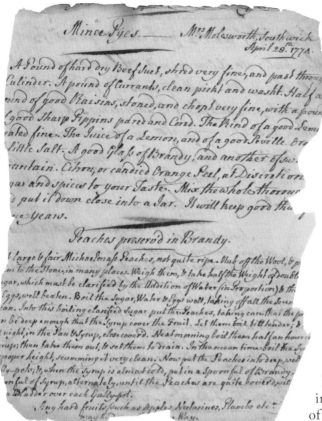

While John and Abigail Adamses' food journey started in their native Massachusetts, they spent time in New York, Philadelphia, Washington, D.C., and Europe, and so their food experiences show the breadth of food culture in those places at that time period.

For example, as the first vice-president for the new nation (a job that he famously found to be "the most insignificant Office that ever the Invention of Man contrived or his Imagination conceived"[9]), John was invited to many dinners in the capital of Philadelphia. In a letter to Abigail in February of 1793, he wrote,

In the Adamses' time, meals were served during the early morning hours and in the afternoon. The latter meals were considered dinner, but were also known as mid-day fare. Evening hours were used for family leisure, studying, or social gathering.

As the first lady, Abigail once wrote to her sister, Mary Smith Cranch, about maintaining her "old habits."

The hospitality of Philadelphia would have kept me, the whole Winter at Dinner with one Family and at Tea and Cards with another: but I have made it a rule to decline all Invitations excepting such as came from Families where I had never dined before, and excepting once with the senators who have families here, once with our Ministers of State and once with foreign Ministers. It has been Employment enough to write Apologies in Answer to invitations. I should have been down with the Ague long before now if I had accepted Invitations to Evening Parties. I never dine out without loosing the next nights Sleep, which shews that there is still a disposition to a fever.[10]

I keep up my old Habit of rising at an early hour. If I did not I should have little command of my Time. At 5 I rise. From that time till 8 I have a few leisure hours. At 8 I breakfast, after which until Eleven I attend to my Family arrangements. At that hour I dress for the day. From 12 until two I receive company, sometimes until 3. We dine at that hour unless on company days which are Tuesdays & Thursdays. After dinner I usually ride out until seven.[8]

A note on dinnerware

Eating foods with hands was a common practice in all social classes. The English settlers who came to the Massachusetts Bay ate primarily with their hands, as did their neighbors, the Native

Bullet molds such as this one were used by the wives of patriots, including Abigail Adams, to melt down pewter ware and make ammunition for the war for independence. *Courtesy of National Park Service, Adams National Historical Park.*

high treason. If a person were to be caught by British soldiers, he or she would be hanged.

As the Adams family gained more wealth and prominence, their dinnerware changed. While in Europe, John became interested in Chinese exports. He purchased several sets of china and sent them home to Massachusetts. Abigail sold most of them, making a profit by doubling or tripling the selling price. The family kept one set and would use it throughout Adams's career as vice president and president. John commissioned a design for the dishes to mark them as the official White House diningware. Unfortunately, the design was never added because of his defeat in the 1800 election.

While in Europe as an envoy representing the United States, John Adams purchased sets of silverware for the family. Because silverware was expensive and he used his own money for the purchases, Adams bought used pieces. He stored the silverware in boxes like this one. *Courtesy of National Park Service, Adams National Historical Park.*

Americans. During John and Abigail's childhoods, they dined with wooden bowls and pewter spoons, which were popular with the early colonists. Pewterware was easily produced because of its low melting point and had been in use since the middle ages. Many early colonists, including John Adams's ancestors, brought pewter from their native country into the New World.

When the Revolutionary War came, family members—including John and Abigail's son, the young John Quincy—recollected that Abigail melted the family pewter ware to make bullets for the patriotic cause. It was dangerous to participate in such an activity and considered

Realizing that reselling sets of china might be a lucrative business, Abigail asked her husband to send her extra sets from Europe. After joining her husband in London, they purchased this set for his role as Ambassador to the Court of St, James. They would later use it for dinners in the United States. *Courtesy of National Park Service, Adams National Historical Park.*

John also purchased silverware for the family while he was in Europe, paying for it out of his own pocket.

Food during war time

Abigail wrote to her husband about the British occupation of Boston, later known as the Siege of Boston, which began in April 1775 after the battles at Lexington and Concord. Some of the Adamses' friends were forced to flee from Boston to Braintree for safety.

But back in Braintree at their family farm, the Adams household suffered from dysentery. The disease, which can lead to death, was easily transmitted by skin-to skin contact and symptoms included high fever, rashes, and diarrhea. Abigail reported to her husband that his brother, Elihu, who was captain of the Braintree Company in the Continental Army, had fallen dangerously ill. He died on August 10, 1775. Abigail fell ill in early September. John and Abigail's youngest son, Thomas, was so ill that he became "pale lean and wan."[11] While Abigail and her son recovered by October, the disease remained prevalent in Boston and in military encampments.

Meanwhile, provisions were scarce.

Trade and commerce had been as important as farming to the New Englanders; they relied heavily on imports. With Parliament's newly passed Coercive Acts, tensions mounted between citizens and British soldiers in occupied Boston. Sea ports were closed and surrounded by the British Navy, which prevented the people who lived in town from receiving goods by ship. Until the troops would evacuate on March 17, 1776, food and supplies were scarce.

These pieces of silverware were purchased by John Adams while he was in Europe. *Courtesy of National Park Service, Adams National Park.*

Even as wood became hard to obtain. Some British troops tore out the wooden pews inside the Old South Meeting House to use them for as firewood (and then used the interior of the building for horse-riding practice).

As Abigail reported:

No Language can paint the distress of the inhabitants, most of them destitute of wood and of provisions of every kind. The Bakers say unless they have a new supply of wood they cannot bake above one fortnight longer—their Bisquit are not above one half the former size… I have heard this Evening that a Man of War has been sent to Falmouth to make a demand of wood, upon which an express was sent of to our camp, and the express says a few hours after he set out, he heard a smart cannonade.[12]

Abigail kept John up to date on the food shortages in Boston:

The present state of the inhabitants of Boston is that of the most abject slaves under the most cruel and despotick of Tyrants. Among many instances I could mention let me relate one. Upon the 17 of june printed hand Bills were pasted up at the corner of streets and upon houses forbideing any inhabitant to go upon their houses or upon any eminence upon pain of death. The inhabitants dared not to look out of their houses nor bee heard or seen to ask a Question. Our prisoners were brought over to the long wharff and there laid all night without any care of their wounds or any resting place but the pavements till the next day, when they exchanged it for the jail, since which we hear they are civily treated. Their living cannot be good, as they can have no fresh provisions. Their Beaf we hear is all gone, and their own wounded men die very fast, so that they have raisd a report that the Bullets were poisond. Fish they cannot have—they have renderd it so difficult to procure it, and the Admiral is such a villan as to oblige every fishing schooner to pay a Dollor every time they go out.[13]

Food shortages also affected the Adams family in Braintree. Abigail wrote, "Grain is what we want ere – meat we may have enough and to spair…We shall very soon have no coffee nor sugar nor pepper here – huckle berrys and milk we are not obliged to commerce for."[14]

The shortages led to desperation:

A poor Milch cow was last week kill'd in Town and sold for a shilling stearling per pound….Every article here in the West india way is very scarce and dear. In six [weeks] we shall not be able to purchase any article of the kind…[15]

And wartime food shortages were made even worse by extreme weather. In November of 1775, Abigail reported:

We have lately had a week of very cold weather, as cold as January, and a flight of snow, which I hope will purify the air of some of the noxious vapours. It has spoild many hundreds of Bushels of Apples, which were designd for cider, and which the great rains had prevented people from making up. Suppose we have lost 5 Barrels by it.[16]

Colonial cookbooks

When the colonies were established in North America, British cookbooks were reprinted in major cities, including Boston and Williamsburg, as standardized texts for upper-class housewives. When the colonies became a nation, people wondered what sort of government that nation should adopt. By ratifying a newly written U.S. Constitution in 1787 and the Bill of Rights in 1791, the notion of individualization took root in America and was reflected culturally in fields such as literature, music, and architecture. Cookbooks also started to address the new American audience. Hannah Glasse's 1747 masterpiece, *The Art of Cookery Made Plain and Easy*, for example, was reprinted in Virginia in 1805 and included a chapter with recipes adapted to the American mode of cooking.

Cookbooks were intended for the upper classes, since they were the only ones who could afford them. Glasse's book was designed as an instruction manual for servants, to save the ladies of the home time in teaching their domestics. The first cookbook by an American author that was published in the United States was *American Cookery* by Amelia Simmons, published in Hartford in 1796. This book included recipes with European origins but also called for new American ingredients, such as blueberries and squash. Such cookbooks served as guides or quick reminders on how to make certain dishes. They also sometimes showed women how to serve a grand, royal-style meal.

Cookbooks in the early nineteenth century might also have sections instructing women on how to sew, clean, and tend to and educate their children. There might be information on home remedies, preserving foods, and canning goods to make "sweetmeats." As Mary Eaton wrote in *The Cook and Housekeeper's Complete and Universal Dictionary* (1823), "The mistress of a family should always remember, that the welfare and good management of the house depend on the eye of the superior…Accounts should be regularly kept…She may consult others who are experienced, and acquaint herself with the necessary quantities of the several articles of family expenditure."[17]

Cookbooks might also have a monthly "Bill of Fare" that would serve as suggestions for what type of dishes to serve for a large dinner. These books offer modern historians an overview on how dinners were served in England and in the colonies. (See Chapter 11.)

At the time, cookbooks did not give precise measurements for ingredients (the first cookbook to use standardized measurements, Fannie Farmer's *The Boston Cooking-School Cook Book*, came out in 1896). Most did not have illustrations to show what the final product would look like. Foods were prepared to a cook's taste. Recipes that were either hand-written or printed in books would only vaguely describe the amounts of spices that might be added.

Recipes in this book

In this work, each recipe is based on the food John and Abigail Adams described in their letters to each other and to other family members, or on foods they might have encountered as noted in John Adams's diary. Each recipe is based on those found in cookbooks that were published during the couple's lifetimes. In this sense, this book is designed to give the reader a broad sense of American culinary culture in the late eighteenth and early nineteenth centuries, both at home and abroad.

For example, John wrote to Abigail in 1775 about one of the dinners that he attended in Philadelphia. He briefly described different kinds of custards that were served. This book includes a few custard recipes as a way to show what John might have eaten at that dinner. (See page 104.)

Recipes have been adapted for modern readers and include standardized measurements. For example, the original recipe for mince pie included suet, which is finely chopped animal fat. For the sake of a modern diet and nutrition, olive oil, canola oil, or margarine are offered as substitutes. Instead of heavy cream, one may use skim milk or light cream. Many of these original recipes contained high levels of cholesterol, saturated fats, and sugar. After all, a large belly, in John Adams's time, was a sign of wealth.

Some ingredients from original recipes were left out because they would be too hard to find today. All the ingredients in this book can be found at farmers markets, supermarkets, and specialty grocery stores. Recipes are also simple and easy to follow for those without a professional knowledge of the culinary arts. In all cases, interpretations of recipes follow the primary sources as closely as possible, but with these nods to today's cooks.

All oven temperatures and food temperatures are given in degrees Fahrenheit.

Finally, a note on spelling in recipes and quotations is offered. The first American dictionary was published by Noah Webster in 1805. In the eighteenth century, spelling was not standardized in writings such as personal letters. In much of their correspondence, both John and Abigail spell words phonetically. For example, one of John Adams' letters, written on December 17, 1798, says, "It is too late for this Cemistry now." Abigail would write Canada as "Canady." Friday was "Fryday." Pie was "pye." Abigail would write, "On tweday Evening I received the Mercury…".[18] Even proper names were sometimes misspelled: Copleys as "Copeleys," for example. All spellings in this book reflect those in the primary sources.

John & Abigail Adams

A TIMELINE

The Early Years:
Massachusetts

Oct. 19, 1735 John Adams born to John Adams, Sr. (also known as Deacon John) and Susanna Boylston Adams in Braintree (now Quincy), Massachusetts). His father is a deacon, farmer, and shoemaker.

Nov. 11, 1744 Abigail Smith born to Rev. William Smith and Elizabeth Quincy in Weymouth, Massachusetts.

1751 John matriculates at Harvard College.

1752 England adopts the Gregorian calendar, shifting dates by 11 days. (In what becomes known as the New Style, John's birthday is adjusted to Oct. 30 and Abigail's to Nov. 22.)

1755 John graduates Harvard and begins teaching in a grammar school in Worcester, Massachusetts.

1758 John is admitted to the Bar at Suffolk County.

1759 John meets Abigail Smith.

May 25, 1761 Deacon John dies, and John inherits the family farm in Braintree.

Oct. 23, 1764 John and Abigail marry after a couple years of courtship.

July 14, 1765 Abigail "Nabby" Adams, first child of John and Abigail, is born.

July 11, 1767 John Quincy Adams, John and Abigail's first son, is born in the home adjacent to his father's birthplace.

December 28, 1768 Susanna Adams, third child of John and Abigail, is born.

Feb. 4, 1770 Susanna, daughter of John & Abigail, dies.

Mar. 05, 1770 The Boston Massacre. Five Boston residents die at the scene, including a runaway slave named Criptus Attucks. Two others die a few days later. The eight British soldiers who fired at the crowd are arrested. John represents the soldiers because he believes everyone should have a fair trial.

May 29, 1770 Birth of Charles Adams, fourth child of John and Abigail.

June 1770 John is elected as a representative to the Massachusetts legislature.

April 1771 John suffers great anxiety while working in Boston. He moves his family back to Braintree.

Sept. 15, 1772 Birth of Thomas Boylston Adams, fifth child of John and Abigail.

The Destruction of Tea at Boston Harbor.
Courtesy of Library of Congress.

Dec. 16, 1773 Boston Tea Party: 92,586 pounds of tea are dumped into Boston Harbor from British ships by colonists who oppose the tea tax.

The Revolutionary War Years:
Politics at home, and then diplomacy in Europe

April 1775 The battles of Lexington and Concord. The colonists take on the most powerful army in the world.

May 1775 The Continental Army is created, and George Washington is named the Commander in Chief.

June 17, 1775 The Battle of Breed's Hill (known as Bunker Hill). Abigail takes her son John Quincy to Penn's Hill to witness the battle.

Mar. 31, 1776 Abigail writes her famous letter, "remember the ladies," to John asking him to include women's rights in new national laws

John Trumbull, *Declaration of Independence, July 4, 1776*. Oil on Canvas, 12'x 18,' 1817. *Courtesy of Yale University Art Gallery.*

July 2, 1776 The Continental Congress unanimously votes for independence.

July 3, 1776 John writes to Abigail from Philadelphia to describe the first Independence Day. "The Second Day of July 1776, will be the most memorable Epocha in the History of America. I am apt to believe that it will be celebrated by succeeding Generations, as the great anniversary Festival...It ought to be solemnized with Pomp and Parade, with Shews, Games, Sports, Guns, Bells, Bonfires and Illuminations from one End of this Continent to the other from this Time forward forever more."

. **July 11, 1777** Elizabeth, last child of John & Abigail, is stillborn.

May 18, 1778 John Adams and Benjamin Franklin write a letter to the American state officials notifying them that eleven British war ships are heading for North America.

October, 1779 People in Massachusetts vote to adopt a Constitution of the Commonwealth. John Adams is the main author of the document, which spells out a government of checks and balances; it is later used to help write the U.S. Constitution.

November 1779 John goes to Europe to negotiate a treaty with England and takes sons John Quincy and Charles with him. They return later in the month.

Feb. 8, 1780 John and John Quincy travel to Paris.

Dec. 20, 1780 John gets the official word from Congress that he has been appointed to go to Holland to negotiate a treaty of amity and commerce.

1781 While in Holland, John sends his two sons, 13-year-old John Quincy and 10-year-old Charles, to attend the University of Leyden.

Sept. 3, 1782 John returns to Paris to join Benjamin Franklin and others in signing the Treaty of Paris, marking an official end to America's War of Independence.

A Diplomat's Life:
John and Abigail in Europe

1784 Abigail and Nabby sail to Europe to join John and John Quincy in France. Abigail's two younger sons, Charles and Thomas, remain at home with Abigail's younger sister, Elizabeth Smith Shaw, and her husband, Rev. John Shaw.

Feb. 24, 1785 John Adams is named as first ambassador to England and meets King George III at the Court of St. James.

1786 John Quincy matriculates at Harvard College.

June 12, 1786 Nabby marries William Stephens Smith, aide-de-camp under General Washington during the American Revolution, in London.

Summer 1786 John and Abigail travel in England and Holland together

July, 1787 The Constitutional Convention is held in Philadelphia. Several prominent figures are absent due to diplomacy abroad, including John Adams and Thomas Jefferson.

1787 John Quincy Adams graduates Harvard College.

April 1788 John and Abigail return to Braintree and move into their new home, called Peace field.

The New Nation:
Executive offices

March 1789 John becomes the first vice-president of the United States, serving with President George Washington. Adams moves to New York City, then the nation's capital, for the job, though he will travel back and forth to Braintree during the year.

Nov. 1790 John moves to Philadelphia, the temporary official U.S. capital from Dec. 1790 until Dec. 1800, when Washington City is established. Abigail joins him briefly then returns to Braintree. He travels back to Braintree over the next several years when Congress is not in session.

1792 The northern part of Braintree, where John Adams was born, is incorporated as the new city of Quincy.

Dec. 1796 Adams is elected president.

March 4, 1797 Adams is inaugurated as the second president of the United States. Abigail joins John in May in Philadelphia.

Nov. 30, 1800 Charles Adams dies in New York City, leaving behind his wife, Sarah "Sally" Smith, and two daughters.

Dec. 1800 Adams is defeated in the presidential election by his old friend, Thomas Jefferson, whom he met in 1775 at the Continental Congress in Philadelphia. The two cease correspondence with each other.

1805 John Quincy becomes a professor of Rhetoric and Oratory at Harvard University.

1811 Thanks to the efforts of Dr. Benjamin Rush, Adams and Jefferson renew their friendship and correspondence.

June 18, 1812 President James Madison declares war on Great Britain, which begins the War of 1812.

August 1813 Nabby dies from breast cancer at her parents' home. She is survived by her husband, William Stephen Smith, newly elected to the U.S. House of Representatives for New York state, and their four children.

Nov. 11, 1818 Abigail Adams succumbs to typhoid fever at Peace field.

At age 27, John Quincy Adams was serving as minister to the Netherlands and engaged to an English-born woman named Louisa Catherine Johnson. It was the same post that his father, John Adams, served when he was 45, just fourteen years earlier. This portrait was painted by the Adamses' family friend John Singleton Copley, a loyalist and a native Bostonian who fled his home just before the Revolutionary War broke out. *Courtesy of Library of Congress, Prints & Photographs Division, Detroit Publishing Company Collection.*

Retirement from public life:
Return to Massachusetts

March 1801 Adams returns to Quincy.

Oct. 5, 1802 John Adams begins writing his autobiography, which will go unfinished.

July 1824-Jan. 1825 Marquis de Lafayette, the last surviving general of the Revolutionary War, visits the United States at the invitation of President James Monroe. He visits John Adams twice at Peace field.

Feb. 9, 1825 John Quincy is elected as President, after a heated and controversial election with Andrew Jackson and three other candidates. The Electoral College is established as a result of this election.

July 4, 1826 On the 50th anniversary of the Declaration of Independence, both John Adams and Thomas Jefferson die. Jefferson dies at about 1 in the afternoon, John about four hours later. He hadn't heard of Jefferson's death and his last words are, "Thomas Jefferson still survives."

Peace field in 1828 by Mrs. G. W. Whitney. *Courtesy of Adams National Historical Park.*

Abigail Adams once wrote that she preferred to be a dairy woman more than anything else. One of her primary responsibilities on the family farm was to make sure there was a good supply of butter. *Photo by Ed Nute. Abigail Adams potrayed by historical reenactor Patricia Bridgman.*

CHAPTER 1

Breakfast

In his diary as a delegate in the Massachusetts legislature, John Adams wrote about a fancy breakfast that made an impression on him:

> This Morning We took Mr. McDougal into our Coach and rode three Miles out of Town, to Mr. Morine Scotts to break fast… A more elegant Breakfast, I never saw—rich Plate—a very large Silver Coffee Pott, a very large Silver Tea Pott—Napkins of the very finest Materials, and toast and bread and butter in great Perfection. After breakfast, a Plate of beautifull Peaches, another of Pairs and another of Plumbs and a Muskmellen were placed on the Table.[1]

Breakfast or "Break-fast" as John Adams would sometimes spell it in his writings, would be served as early as 6 or sometimes as late as 9 in the morning. It was a simple meal to start the day, even if elaborately presented. A breakfast might include bread, butter, cheese, tea, pudding, porridge, cider and sometimes milk. John frequently recalled having bread and cheese or something simple in the morning hours, just as he did in his student days at Harvard. In a letter to Abigail Adams, John recorded:

> About five O Clock this Morning, I went with young Dr. [Thomas] Bond [,Jr.] at his Invitation and in his Carriage, to his Fathers Seat in the Country. We breakfasted, upon balm Tea and Bread and Butter. A most amuzing and refreshing Excursion We had.[2]

Hard cider became New England's favorite drink when the first colonists learn to press apples and turn them into liquids. As John once wrote,

> The Indian Preacher cryed good God!—that ever Adam and Eve should eat that Apple when they knew in their own Souls it would make good Cyder.[3]

Milk could be hard to come by. Like tea and molasses, the price of milk was inflated during times of war. With no refrigeration or pasteurization, getting fresh milk every day could be a challenge, and milk spoiled quickly. In a letter to Abigail, John wrote, "Milk has become the Breakfast of many of the wealthiest and genteelest Families here."[4]

As an ardent patriot striving for his nation to be independent, John Adams hoped to steer his family and fellow citizens away from goods imported by the British East India Company, like tea. He wrote to Abigail about his wish: "I assure you, the best Families in this Place have left off in a great Measure the Use of West India Goods."[5]

When John traveled to Europe as a diplomat, he and his son tried to maintain their breakfast habits. John Quincy would write, "This morning we got up at about 5 o clock we breakfasted upon tea…"[6] There are times, John recorded, "The orders are to breakfast at 10., dine at 5. and sup at 10."[7]

A trip to Spain led to a new breakfast experience: chocolate drink from the Spanish colonies in the New World. In his diary, John recorded:

> Breakfasted for the first time on Spanish Chocolate which fully answered the fame it had acquired in the World. Till that time I had no Idea that any thing that had the Appearance of Chocolate and bore that name could be so delicious and salubrious.[8]

While in Amsterdam, John turned to coffee as an alternative to his New England cider. " My Breakfasts don't relish, for want of a little Plutarch, with the Coffee."[9]

During warmer seasons, some would prefer having fruits for breakfast. In his diary, dated June 7, 1771, Friday, Adams recorded:

> [Colburn] Barrell this Morning at Breakfast entertained Us with an Account of his extravagant Fondness for Fruit. When he lived at New market he could get no fruit but Strawberries, and he used frequently to eat 6 Quarts in a Day. At Boston, in the very hottest of the Weather he breakfasts upon Water Melons—neither Eats nor drinks any Thing else for Breakfast. In the Season of Peaches he buys a Peck, every Morning, and eats more than half of them himself. In short he eats so much fruits in the Season of it that he has very little Inclination to any other Food. He never found any Inconvenience or ill Effect from fruit—enjoys as much Health as any Body. Father Dana is immoderately fond of fruit, and from several other Instances one would conclude it very wholsome.[10]

Food was often prepared by servants in the upper classes. While the Adamses frequently complained about the expense of living away from home, they did manage to hire workers from their neighbors to tend their farm and prepare their meals.

Coffee was served at breakfast and throughout the day. As the wife of the first vice president for the United States, Abigail wrote in 1793:

> I could wish if You must go to Philadelphia that You could have gone immediatly to your old Lodgings, Brisler could make Breakfast and coffe in the afternoon even if you was provided with dinner in some other place.[11]

The recipes in this chapter give an idea of the kinds of breakfast foods John Adams enjoyed while he was a Continental Congress representative for Massachusetts and later, when he served as president of the United States.

But first, a note on butter.

Butter: Essential for cooking and survival

As a housewife in the eighteenth century, it was important to make the finest butter for the family. During war time on the home front, one of Abigail's responsibilities was to create a sustainable amount of butter. In one of her letters to John Adams, she wrote:

> I live as I never did before, but I am not agoing to complain... I shall fat Beaf and pork enough, make butter and cheesse enough. I should do exceeding well if we could but keep the money good, but at the rate we go on I know not what will become of us.[12]

Butter played a major role in most English dishes, and eighteenth-century women like Abigail learned how to churn butter at an early age. During their frequent separations, Abigail would nag her husband:

> If my dear Friend you will promise to come home, take the Farm into your own hands and improve it, let me turn dairy woman, and assist you in getting our living this way; instead of running away to foreign courts and leaving me half my Life to mourn in widowhood, then I will run you in debt for this Farm...[13]

While away from home, John and Abigail frequently kept each other informed on the price of butter. When John was in Philadelphia, he reported:

> Price current.—Oak Wood £4:15s:od. Pr. Cord. Bad Beer, not so good as your Small Beer, 15d: Pr. Quart. Butter one Dollar Pr. Pound. Beef 2s:6d. Coffee a dollar a Pound. Bohea 8 dollars. Souchong £4: 10s. Hyson £6. Mean brown sugar 6s. 6d. a pound. Loaf sugar 18s. a pound. Rum 45s. a Gallon. Wine 2 dollars a Bottle.[14]

When John sailed across the Atlantic as an envoy to Europe, butter was an essential but was in rare supply. As he passed through parts of Europe he witnessed "Signs of Poverty and Misery, among the People...Nothing appears rich but the Churches..." In his diary, John recorded:

> We are obliged, in this Journey to carry our own Beds, Blanketts, Sheets, Pillows &c., our own Provisions of Chocolat, Tea, Sugar, Meat, Wine, Spirits, and every Thing that We want. We get nothing at the Taverns, but Fire, Water, and Salt. We carry our own Butter, Cheese, and indeed Salt and Pepper too.[15]

Butter was not only valuable for household use, but also could be sold for cash. During times of war, this could be especially important.

Abigail reported on the inflationary price of butter in a letter to John in 1777.

> ...That a Scarcity prevails of every article not only of Luxery, but even the necessaries of life is a certain fact. Every thing bears an exorbitant price. The act which for a while was in some measure regarded and stemed the torrent of oppression is now no more Heeded than if it had never been made; Indian Corn at 5 shillings, Rye 11 and 12 shilling[s], but none scarcly to be had even at that price, Beaf 8 pence, veal 6 pence and 8 pence, Butter 1 & 6 pence...[16]

While John was abroad in 1779, Abigail again reported on the high price of butter:

> You had as good tell me to procure Diamonds for them, and when Bills will fetch but five for one, hard Money will exchange ten — which I think is very provoking and I must give at the rate of ten and sometime 20 for one for every article I purchase. I blush whilst I give you a price current, all Butchers meat from a Dollor to 8 shillings per pound, corn 25 Dollars, Rye 30 per Bushel, flower 50 pounds per hundred, potatoes ten dollors per Bushel, Butter 12 shillings per pound, cheese 8, Sugar 12 shillings per pound, Molasses 12 Dollors per Gallon, Labour 6 and 8 Dollors a Day, a common Cow from 60 to 70 pound, and all English goods in proportion... This is our present situation. ...I have and do study every method of oeconomy in my power, otherways a mint of money would not support a family.[17]

During John Adams's vice presidency in New York City, Abigail tried to make herself at home by asking John for "all the butter which can be procured."[18] With the high cost of living in New York, Abigail insisted on getting butter from her native state, for a cheaper price, instead of buying it locally.

Since early New Englanders had difficulty growing wheat to produce flour, they turned to alternative ingredients for bread making. Buckwheat originated in Northern England and made its way to some of the colonies including New England and Pennsylvania.[19] In his journal, John Adams recorded on Wednesday, September 21, 1774:

> Captn. Callender came to breakfast with US. Coll. Dagworthy and his Brother Captn. Dagworthy breakfasted with Us. Mrs. Yard entertained Us, with Muffins, Buck Wheat Cakes and common Toast. Buckwheat is an excellent grain, and is very plenty here.[20]

The following recipe is based on Amelia Simmons' cookbook *American Cookery* (1796). It makes about 6 pancakes.

1 (¼-ounce) package yeast
½ teaspoon sugar
¾ cup buckwheat flour
1 cup buttermilk
butter or cooking oil spray

Dissolve the package of yeast in 1/3 cup of warm water (temperature around 110 degrees) with the sugar.

Whisk the yeast, flour, and buttermilk together in a large mixing bowl. Do not overmix.

Spray cooking oil on a skillet or a large pan, or melt butter in the pan. Pour the batter into a 4-inch disk. Let it cook for about 2-3 minutes and then flip it to cook the other side. Repeat until you use all the batter.

Serve with additional butter.

The kind of muffins Adams referred to in his journal entry would be called English muffins today.

They were introduced to America from Wales in the mid-eighteenth century. Yeast often came from ale-yeast. An alternative would be barm, which is foam from the top of a fermented alcoholic drink.

This recipe is based on Maria Eliza Ketelby Rundell's *A New System of Domestic Cookery* (1823 edition) and the *Cookery Reformed: Or, the Lady's Assistant,* which was published in 1755 and had an anonymous author.

Butter to grease pan,
   plus more to brush on muffins
2 ½ cups all purpose flour
1 large egg, beated
1 cup whole milk, warm
1 package of yeast, prepared according to directions on package

Preheat the oven to 350 degrees. Grease a sheet pan.

Mix flour, egg, milk, and yeast in a large bowl. Knead them briefly until they become not-sticky. This is a soft dough. Do not overflour during the kneading process.

Divide the dough into small circular disks (about 1 to 2 inches thick). Place them on agreased sheet pan.

Put the pan in the oven. Brush some melted butter on top of the muffins. Bake for about 30 minutes (until you notice the smell of fresh baked bread).

As Mary Eaton wrote in *The Cook and Housekeeper's Complete and Universal Dictionary* (1823), "Muffins should be not be cut, but pulled open." Serve with butter.

In 1766, John Adams mentioned biscuits in his diary:

> "I was invited by Crafts and Trott, to go and spend an Evening with them and some others, Avery was mentioned to me as one. I went, and was very civilly and respectfully treated, by all Present. We had Punch, Wine, Pipes and Tobacco, Bisquit and Cheese — &c. They Chose a Committee to make Preparations for grand Rejoicings upon the Arrival of the News of a Repeal of the Stamp Act, and I heard afterwards they are to have such Illuminations, Bonfires, Piramids, Obelisks, such grand Exhibitions, and such Fireworks, as were never before seen in America. — I wish they mayn't be disappointed."[21]

Less than a decade later, in October of 1775, Abigail described the hardships that the town of Boston endured during the Seige of Boston and the occupation by the British troops, including the diminished size of biscuits due to food shortages.

> The Bakers say unless they have a new supply of wood they cannot bake above one fortnight longer —their Bisquit are not above one half the former size. The Soldiers are obliged to do very hard duty, and are uneasy to a great degree, many of them declareing they will not continue much longer in such a state but at all hazards will escape; the inhabitants are desperate, and contriveing means of escape.[22]

The following recipe is based on a combination of recipes from several works, including Susannah Carter's *The Frugal Housewife: Or, Complete Woman Cook* (1796 edition), Amelia Simmons's *American Cookery* (1796), and John Farley's *The London Art of Cookery* (1811 edition).

2 ½ cups flour, sifted
2 sticks of softened, unsalted butter, plus more to grease pan
2 eggs, beaten

Preheat oven to 375 degrees.

Grease a sheet pan with butter.

In a large mixing bowl, sift the flour and break the butter into cubes. Mix them together until it looks like oatmeal.

Then in a separate bowl, beat the eggs. Pour them into the flour mixture. Mix until it gets thick. Knead the mixture briefly in the bowl before transferring to a floured surface.

On the floured surface, press dough down to about ¼-inch thick. Use a cookie cutter to cut the dough into round disks. Place the biscuits on the sheet pan. Bake for 10-15 minutes. Serve with butter.

As Maria Eliza Ketelby Rundell wrote in her *A New System of Domestic Cookery* (1823 edition), "Cocoa—Is a light wholesome breakfast."[23]

While in Spain, John Adams wrote in his diary on December 10, 1779, about this "salubrious" drink that was brought from the Spanish colonies in the Americas.[24]

Chocolate had been sacred to the Aztecs and Mayans for thousands of years. When the Spanish conquistadors arrived in what would later be known as Mexico, they seized many treasures including chocolate, which they took back to Europe. Soon, this "food of the gods" became a popular drink among Western Europeans. Major cities began to produce and sell chocolate.

John wrote to his daughter, Nabby, about this treat:

I have met with few Things more remarkable than the Chocolate which is the finest I ever saw. I will enquire whether it is the Superiour Quality of the Cocoa Nut, or any other Ingredient which they intermix with it, or a better Art of making it, which renders it so much superiour to any other.[25]

John also observed how the Spanish women drank chocolate:

1779. DECEMBER 22. WEDNESDAY. Drank Tea, at Senior Lagoaneres. Saw the Ladies drink Chocolat in the Spanish Fashion. A Servant brought in a Salver, with a Number of Tumblers, of clean, clear Glass, full of cold Water, and a Plate of Cakes, which were light Pieces of Sugar. Each Lady took a Tumbler of Water and a Piece of Sugar, dipped her Sugar in her Tumbler of Water, eat the one and drank the other. The Servant then brought in another Salver, of Cups of hot Chocolat. Each Lady took a Cup and drank it, and then Cakes and bread and Butter were served. Then each Lady took another cup of cold Water and here ended the Repast.[26]

A letter from Abigail Adams to her daughter-in-law, Ann ("Nancy) Harrod Adams, on August 28, 1806, requesting some chocolate for the household. Original manuscript from Adams All Generations. *Courtesy of Massachusetts Historical Society.*

The customs for consuming chocolate were different among European countries. The Spanish mixed it with milk and spices. The French enjoyed chocolate as a drink, too, and later invented a new dessert known as mousse.

Some would add other spices and even alcohol into the chocolate drink. For example, in Frederick Nutt's *The Complete Confectioner, Or, The Whole Art of Confectionary*, reprinted in America in 1807, is this recipe for chocolate:

> No. 243. Chocolate: FOR four bottles of brandy, take one pound of the best chocolate, cut in small bits, a little salt, two cloves, and a little cinnamon; you are to infuse all in the brandy; two pounds of sugar clarified in two bottles and half a pint of water, with whites of eggs, and filter it through the paper.

Chocolate became so popular that Spanish painter Luis Egidio Meléndez (1715-1780) interpreted the drink in his painting, *Still Life with Chocolate Service, Bread Roll, and Biscuits* (1770). As the painting suggests, chocolate drinks were commonly served with bread. This is a perfect example of what John Adams would have experienced and enjoyed during his time in Spain.

The earliest written recipe by a European on chocolate was published in 1631 by Antonio Colmenero de Ledesma as "Chocolate, or, An Indian Drinke." The author described how different spices added to a chocolate drink could be remedies for various illnesses:

> Set a Pot of Conduit Water over the fire untill it boiles, then to every person that is to drink, put an ounce of Chocolate, with as much Sugar into another Pot; wherein you must poure a pint of the said boiling Water, and therein mingle the Chocolate and the Sugar, with the instrument called El Molinillo, untill it be thoroughly incorporated: which done, poure in as many halfe pints of the said Water as there be ounces of Chocolate, and if you please, you may put in one or two yelks of fresh Eggs, which must be beaten untill they froth very much; the hotter it is drunke, the better it is, being cold it may doe harme. You may likewise put in a slice of white bred or Bisquet, and eate that with the Chocolate. The newer and fresher made it is, the more benefit you shall finde by it; that which comes from forreigne parts, and is stale, is not so good as that which is made here. [27]

Nearly two hundred years later, another recipe for chocolate drink appeared in Mary Eaton's *The Cook and Housekeeper's Complete and Universal Dictionary* (1823). The author noted, "If not make too thick this will form a very good breakfast or supper."

The following recipe is an interpretation of one of the Adams family's favorite drinks.

About 1 cup of chocolate pieces (99% cocoa)
4 tablespoons milk
About 5 tablespoons sugar

In a pan, bring ¾ cup of water to a boil. Reduce to medium heat. Add the chocolate, and stir until melted. Add the milk and sugar, and stir.

Despite the rocky soil at Peace field, the home in Massachusetts into which they moved in 1788, John and Abigail grew vegetables and berries, including strawberries. In 1794, John wrote to Abigail, "Tell Brisler to preserve me a quart or two of Strawberries if he Stays till Strawburry time."[28] In May of 1798, Abigail wrote to her older sister, Mary Smith Cranch, "And my strawberry bed Stutson [Stetson] must attend to very soon in the Spring."[29]

Strawberries were abundant throughout New England. Housewives made sauces and preserves from them and from other types of berries, such as gooseberries and red currants. This sample recipe is based on Mary Randolph's *The Virginia Housewife*, first published in 1824.

1 pound strawberries
¼ pound gooseberries (optional)
About 3 tablespoon sugar, to taste

Get the largest strawberries before they are too ripe. Remove the stems and wash the berries. Slice them in halves.

Remove stems from gooseberries, if using, and wash berries.

In a saucepan, place half the strawberries and crush with a potato smasher. Then do the same for the other half and for the gooseberries, if using.

Turn up heat, stirring berries to keep them from sticking to the bottom of the pan. Slowly add sugar to sweeten the mixture. Boil at high heat for about 10 minutes, continuing to stir.

When the mixture becomes sauce, remove from the heat, cover, and let cool. Store in a sterile glass jar with a sealed top. Refrigerate.

Photo by Ed Nute

CHAPTER 2

Bread

Bread did not play a major role in the Adamses' diet for several reasons. First, baking bread was time consuming and the process could heat up the house too quickly on warm days. It was also difficult to grow wheat in the New England climate. In fact, the early settlers were subject to a law limiting the use of flour to special occasions such as elections and weddings. While that law was long abolished by the Adamses' time period, New Englanders were in the habit of bread baking just once a week. And during war time, it was especially important to economize food supplies and limit bread making.

Rye and corn breads were popular alternatives to wheat bread. While corn was a native plant, rye was introduced to the New World from England.[1] Bread was served at breakfast and at other meals, but it was not common, and both John and Abigail mentioned it in their writings. In his autobiography, John wrote:

> The House had been the Habitation of military Guards, and was as dirty as a stable: but his Lordship had prepared a large handsome Room, by spreading a Carpet of Moss and green Spriggs from Bushes and Shrubbs in the Neighbourhood, till he had made it not only wholesome but romantically elegant, and he entertained Us with good Claret, good Bread cold Ham, Tongues and Mutton.[2]

In his diary, in 1771, he recorded having wheat bread while traveling:

> In all this Ramble from Stafford, I have met with nobody that I knew, excepting Jo. Trumble, who with his father the Governor were crossing the ferry for the East Side when

I was for the West. Bespoke Entertainment for the Sabbath, at Shalers, and drank Tea. She brought me in the finest and sweetest of Wheat Bread, and Butter, as yellow as Gold, and fine Radishes, very good Tea and sugar. I regaled without Reserve. But my Wife is 150 Miles from me at least, and I am not yet homeward bound. I wish Connecticutt River flowed through Braintree. But the barren rocky Mountains of Braintree are as great a Contrast as can be conceived to the level smoth, fertile Plains of this Country. Yet Braintree pleases me more.[3]

During the war, Abigail once wrote to her husband about the shortage of bread:

> We have had a most uncommon hot and dry season. The months of july and August were the hottest ever known here and have cut of our corn, our potatoes and every other article. The cry for Bread is such as I never heard before. Rye 10 dollors a Bushel, Barly 6, corn not to be had, not one Barrel of cider will be made upon this place this year.[4]

Abigail gave her definition of bread to her granddaughter Caroline Smith on August 6, 1812, "Bread, the staff of life and the chief reliance of the poor."[5]

Eighteenth-century bread recipes often used the word "leven," showing that yeast was used to make the bread. Yeast, of course, was not available for purchase in those days and had to be made by home cooks.

During Abigail's years as First Lady, she hosted gatherings for government officials and other guests. In March 31, 1798, she wrote to her sister Mary Smith Cranch about hosting a gathering of "44 Gentlemen" in Philadelphia:

> Inclosed I sent you a specimin of the Manners, Religion & politeness of one of the 44 Gentlemen, who can come and Eat of my Bread, & drink of my wine, one whom the Virginians consider as a Paragon of politeness, whom they have plumed themselves upon as a promising Man, and a man of Property, one of their best speakers.[6]

Although she did not specifically record what type of bread was baked for such an engagement, the following recipes from the era show the types of breads she and John Adams enjoyed during their lifetimes.

When Deacon John Adams died on May 25, 1761, John inherited a cottage that was just 75 feet from his birthplace. He modified the kitchen fireplace with new equipment and a bread oven. A room next to the kitchen was used for dry goods storage, including flour. Abigail would use a table, like this one, for mixing dough and preparing food. She also taught her children to read while she cooked and taught them to recite Latin phrases.

Brown Wheat Bread

In John Adams's diary of June 30, 1770, a few months after the Boston Massacre, he made an allusion to what a loaf of brown bread might look like:

> I forgot Yesterday to mention, that I stopped and enquired the Name of a Pond, in Wenham, which I found was Wenham Pond, and also the Name of a remarkable little Hill at the mouth of the Pond, which resembles a high Loaf of our Country brown Bread, and found that it is called Peters's Hill to this day, from the famous Hugh Peters, who about the Year 1640 or before, preached from the Top of that Hillock, to the People who congregated round the Sides of it, without any Shelter for the Hearers, before any Buildings were erected, for public Worship.[7]

Brown bread was also known as "household bread" and sometimes called "wheaten brown bread." It could be used as an ingredient for other dishes, such as soup or pot stew. In some cases, leftovers of brown bread could be used for making pies or stuffing.

In 1805, Abraham Edlin published *A Treatise on the Art of Bread-making*, which offered tips on successful baking at home and included a recipe for making "brown wheat bread," from which this recipe has been adapted.

Butter to grease pan
2 ½ cups warm water (about 110 degrees)
1 package yeast
3 ½ cups whole wheat flour
1 tablespoon salt
flour

Preheat the oven to 350 degrees. Grease a bread pan.

In a small bowl, prepare the yeast according to the directions on the package.

Mix the flour and salt in a large mixing bowl, and then stir in the yeast water.

On a working surface, spread some flour, and then knead the dough for about 10 minutes.

Place the dough in a 10-inch bread pan and bake for 30 minutes.

In 1817, Henry Bradshaw Fearon visited the Adamses from England. He recorded what he ate during that special visit.

> 1st course a pudding made of Indian corn, molasses and butter, 2nd, veal, bacon, neck of mutton, potatoes, cabbages, carrots and Indian beans, Madeira wine, of which each drank two glasses. We sat down to dinner at one o'clock. At two nearly all went a second time to church. For tea we had pound cake, wheat bread and butter, and bread made out of Indian corn and rye.[8]

Richard Parkinson toured America and in 1805 published his experiences. He wrote that Americans "cannot make bread as in England," but he was fascinated by their bread making with Indian corn flour and yeast. He recorded the new idea of mixing sugar or molasses, bran and water, boiled with "a small quantity of hops…worked up with flour…."Parkinson also noted "Indian corn bread" was widely "habituated" and "is in use on every occasion." [9]

The following is loosely based on a bread recipe from Abraham Edlin's *A Treatise on the Art of Bread-making* (1805).

1 package yeast
2 ½ cups of warm water
2 ½ cups yellow corn meal
2 ½ cups rye flour
flour
butter for pan

Preheat the oven to 350 degrees.

In a small bowl, prepare the yeast by mixing it with the warm water.

In another mixing bowl, sift the rye flour and yellow corn meal together through a sieve.
Whisk in the yeast water.

Flour the surface you are working on, then knead the dough for about 8 to 10 minutes. Place the dough in a bread pan greased with butter and bake for about 10 minutes.

Serve with butter or strawberry preserves.

Abigail Adams used a table like this one for mixing dough and preparing food. She also taught her children how to read while she worked at the kitchen table. *Courtesy of National Park Service, Adams National Historical Park.*

Reflector ovens were frequently used for cooking meat such as leg of lamb or a chicken. Radiant heat helped the meat to cook evenly. *Courtesy National Park Service, Adams National Historical Park.*

CHAPTER 3

Meat and Poultry

British colonists ate meat and poultry, relying both on wild animals and farm animals such as chickens, sheep, cows, and pigs. In New England, towns constructed "hogrccvcs" to keep the pigs under control. Farmers salted the pork for the winter season since there was no refrigeration.

Both John and Abigail Adams mentioned meat quite often in their correspondence.

On one occasion, John wrote about a mutton dinner with Colonel Josiah Quincy:

> At one of the Clock we took our Mutton and Cyder, under the shade of a fine Tree, and laid our Provisions on a large flat stone which answered for Table, Dish and Plate, and then we dined expecting with much Pleasure an easy sail Home before the Wind, which then bread fresh at East.[1]

Once, in France, he wrote about some particularly good pork and bacon.

> We found the Pork and Bacon, this day, as We had often found them before, most excellent and delicious, which surprized me the more, as I had always thought the Pork in France very indifferent, and occasioned my Inquiry into the manner of raising it. The Chief justice informed me, that much of it was fatted upon Chesnutts, and much more upon Indian Corn which was much better. That in some Provinces of Spain they had a peculiar kind of Acorns growing upon old pasture Oaks, which were very sweet and produced better Pork than either Chesnuts or Indian Corn That there were parts of Spain, where they fatted hogs upon Vipers. They commonly cutt off their heads and gave the Bodies to their Swine and they produced better Pork, than Chesnuts, Indian Corn or Acorns. That the Swine were so fond of these Vipers that they would attack them when they would find them alive, put one of their fore feet upon the head and hold it down while they eat the Body, but would not eat the head. That they were so expert at this Art, that they very rarely got stung by them.[2]

Wildlife and various domesticated animal parts would be consumed as delicacies. Up to the late nineteenth century, many cookbooks included instructions on how to prepare "neat's tongue" (cow tongue), pigeon pie, sheep's trottles, and rabbit meat. Both John and Abigail wrote about having turtle soup. Abigail once recieved a 114-pound turtle as a gift, and she made a soup with it. As her daughter Nabby wrote:

> We received a Card from Capt. [John] Hay, who has just arrived from the West Indies, and a Present of a Turtle weighing about an hundred weight. This came very opportunely as, your father had invited all the Foreign Ministers and my Lord Carmarthen to dine with him next fryday, and such a Dish as this will not be improper, upon such an occasion.[3]

Frequently, John and Abigail would write to each other about mince pies. In one letter he described such a dinner.

> Saturday I dined with him in Company with Brigadier Prebble, Major Freeman and his son, &c. and a very genteel Dinner we had. Salt Fish and all its apparatus, roast Chickens, Bacon, Pees, as fine a Salad as ever was made, and a rich meat Pie-Tarts and Custards &c., good Wine and as good Punch as ever you made. A large spacious, elegant House, Yard and Garden &c. I thought I had got into the Palace of a Nobleman. After Dinner when I was obliged to come away, he renewed his Invitation to me to make his House my Home, whenever I should come to Town again.[4]

He enjoyed the dish when he was in Europe, too:

> Two Irish Gentlemen came to pay their Respects to me, Michael Meagher Oreilly and Lewis Obrien. Obrien afterwards sent me a Meat Pie and a minced Pie and two Bottles of Frontenac Wine, which gave Us a fine Supper.[5]

Mince pie was invented in medieval times. The pies often included some of the less desirable parts of an animal, including internal organs and animal fats (suet). It was a common practice to preserve meat and spices in stone jars in the wintertime and use it for these pies, combining it with fruits and more spices.

The pie became a holiday favorite, and the English brought the recipe with them to the New World. It was popular on days of thanksgiving.

On January 16th, 1795, Abigail wrote to her "Dearest Friend":

> Master Cleverly is in great distress that the President, being a Church Man, should appoint a Thanksgiving during Lent. He shakes his Head, and says tis a very Arbitary thing. I suppose he cannot help connecting plumb pudding, Roast Turkey and Minced Pye.[6]

Photo by Ed Nute

The following recipe, adapted for modern palates, is based on Anonymous' *Cookery Reformed: Or, the Lady's Assistant* (1755).

For the pie crust, refer to this book's recipe for Cherry Pie (see page 108), or use a premade pie crust from the grocery store.

1 ½ pounds ground beef (85% lean)
1 large apple, finely chopped
½ cup raisins
¾ cup sugar
1 ½ teaspoons ground mace
2 tablespoons ground nutmeg
1 ½ teaspoons ground cloves
¼ cup dried currants
1 tablespoon lemon juice
Peels from ½ an orange, grated
egg white

Preheat oven to 450 degrees.

In a large pan, over medium high heat, cook the ground beef until well done.

Once the beef cools down, mix it with the other ingredients, except the lemon juice and orange peel.

Put the mixture in a glass jar or tightly sealed plastic container. Refrigerate overnight to let the flavors meld.

Place a pie crust in a pie pan. Fill the pie crust with the mixture. Sprinkle the lemon juice and grated orange peels on top of the mixture. Top with another pie crust and seal the edges by moistening with a few drops of water.

Mix egg white and water in a small bowl to create a wash. Brush the surface with the wash.

Place pie in the oven and bake for about 25 minutes. Use a knife to poke through the center to check for doneness.

As a delegate to the Continental Congress, John Adams dined at numerous homes on his trips to Philadelphia from Braintree.

On November 17, 1777, he wrote in his diary about a meal with the Brewster family in Orange County, New York, whom he found to be much like New Englanders.

> The Manners of this Family are exactly like those of the N.E. People. A decent Grace before and after Meat-Fine Pork and Beef and Cabbage and Turnip.[7]

This recipe for beef and cabbage is based on the Frugal Dishes section in John Farley's work, *The London Art of Cookery* (1811 edition).

Adams grew cabbage in his own garden. In 1815, in a letter to Vander Kemp, he wrote: "I raised in my garden last year 'Cossack Cabbages' incomparably the finest I have ever seen."[8]

For this dish, use large pieces of cabbage. Beef stew chunks work best; cut the meat into smaller pieces if desired.

1 pound beef stew chunks
1 ½ tablespoons table salt
2 tablespoons unsalted butter, plus more for pot
½ cabbage
1 teaspoon ground white pepper

Wash the beef stew chunks, then salt the meat. Let it sit for an hour or two in a sealed plastic bag.

Rub butter on the inside of a large pot or dutch oven.
Peel the cabbage into large pieces. Set them at the bottom of the pan. Sprinkle with white pepper.

Placed the salted beef on top of the cabbage. Then place a few more large pieces of cabbage on top of the beef. Fill the pan with about 5 to 6 cups of water, until the water covers the top layer of cabbage.

Cover the pan, and cook at medium-high heat for about 40 minutes, until the meat is tender, but not red. Serve on a large plate, placing the meat on top of the cabbage.

One entry in John Adams' diary, dated November 18, 1777, includes a mention of salt pork and cabbage.

> Lodged at Brooks's, 5 Miles from the North River. Rode to the Continental Ferry, crossed over, and dined at Fish Kill, at the Drs. Mess, near the Hospital, with Dr. Sam. Adams, Dr. Eustis, Mr. Wells, &c. It was a feast—Salt Pork and Cabbage, roast Beef and Potatoes, and a noble suit Pudding, Grog and a Glass of Port.[9]

The following recipe is based on *French Domestic Cookery, by an English Physician,* penned by an anonymous author in 1825. When choosing salted pork, use the lean portion for the dish, but don't cut off the fat. As the meat boils, the fat will make broth.

  4 or 5 cups of water
  ¼ pound organic salted pork, chopped into pieces
  3 or 4 large pieces of cabbage
  freshly ground pepper

Bring the water to a boil in a large pot, then add the chopped, salted pork and pieces of cabbage.

Reduce heat and let meat simmer for about 2 hours. As the mixture boils, add some freshly ground pepper.

Plate the salt pork and cabbage. The broth can serve as soup.

While in Holland, negotiating with Dutch bankers for a loan of five million guilders to fund the War of Independence for the British Colonies, John Adams dined with European diplomats. But it was clear that he missed meals at home with family.

On August 31, 1782, John wrote to his wife:

> I am going to Dinner with a Duke and a Dutchess and a Number [of] Ambassadors and Senators, in all the Luxury of this luxurious World: but how much more luxurious it would be to me, to dine upon roast beef with Parson Smith,[78] Dr. Tufts or Norton Quincy—or upon rusticrat Potatoes with Portia—Oh! Oh! Hi ho hum—and her Daughter and sons.[10]

(Parson Smith was Abigail's father; Dr. Cotton Tufts was her uncle, and Norton Quincy another uncle. Portia was Abigail's nickname.)

These recipes interpret the roast beef meal John Adams was dreaming of in his letter to Abigail. They are based on those in Mary Eaton's *The Cook and Housekeeper's Complete and Universal Dictionary* (1823).

For the roast beef:
    4 tablespoons unsalted butter, softened
    3-pound boneless rump roast
    A few pinches of salt
    1 tablespoon flour
    Horseradish

Line a sheet pan or roast pan with aluminum foil. Rub it with butter.

Preheat the oven to 325 degrees.

Rinse the meat. Dry it with a white paper towel.

Place the meat in the roasting pan, then cook for about 45 minutes, until the meat is half-way done.

Take the meat out of the oven. Spread some butter on it, and sprinkle it with a little bit of flour. Put the meat back into the oven and let it cook for 45 minutes.
(Cooking time is about 30 minutes per pound at 325 degrees).

Toward the end, lower the oven temperature to 250 degrees. Check the meat to make sure it is almost well done. For medium rare, the internal temperature should be 145 degrees. The meat can be a little pink. Do not over cook.

Slice, and serve with horseradish.

For the gravy:

¼ onion, chopped
2 carrots, sliced
¼ turnip, chopped
3 stalks of celery, sliced
2 cups water
2 teaspoons vegetable oil, or unsalted butter (or grease from 3 strips of cooked bacon)
1 tablespoon flour
½ teaspoon salt
1 teaspoon ground allspice

If using bacon grease, cook bacon first and reserve grease.

In a large pot, boil the vegetables in 2 cups water for about 15 to 20 minutes.

Strain the vegetables from the broth. Put broth in a new pan and heat to simmering. Then slowly add oil/butter/grease and flour and stir to thicken.

Add salt and allspice, to taste. Stir.

For the boiled potatoes:

4 large potatoes
Water
¼ cup of table salt

Soak the potatoes in a large bowl of cold water for about an hour.

Use a scrubbing pad to gently scrub the dirt from the potatoes. Be careful not to scrub off the peels.

Fill a sauce pan with about 3½ cups cold water. Set it at medium heat. When the water begin to boil, put the potatoes into the pan.

After 15 minutes, add the salt to the pan and 4 more cups of water.

When the potatoes are done, remove them from the water. Gently peel the skins.

Abigail Adams wrote to her sister Mary Smith Cranch on Sunday, July 25, 1784: "We had a handsome dinner of salt fish pea soup Boild fowl and tongue roast and fry'd lamb, with pudding and fruit."[11]

Fried lamb can be served with a side vegetable, such as boiled peas or sliced carrots. This recipe uses lamb steak, which can be found in a grocery store. If you want to serve it in smaller portions, use lamb shoulder arm chops. Each slice is about one-quarter pound and 1-inch thick. In most stores, lamb steaks and other forms of lamb chops are already chopped into thick slices (usually about 1-inch thick) and wrapped separately. Use cuts with or without the bones.

This recipe is based on an Hannah Glasse's *The Art of Cookery Made Plain and Easy* (1784 edition) and T. Williams' *The Accomplished Housekeeper, and Universal Cook* (1797).

1 to 2 sticks margarine (or use canola oil)
3 pounds lamb steak (or shoulder arm chops)
4 ½ tablespoons nutmeg
2 tablespoons dried marjoram
2 tablespoons dried thyme
1 tablespoon winter savory
3 ½ teaspoons table salt
¼ cup of all-purpose flour
4 teaspoons ground black pepper
1 cup bread crumbs
4 egg yolks
Dried parsley as garnish
1 lemon, sliced

Put margarine in skillet and set on stove at medium high heat.

Wash the meat. Dry it with paper towel.

Mix spices, salt, flour, pepper and bread crumbs in a large bowl.

Dip the meat in the egg yolks, then coat the meat with the dried mixture.

When the oil is hot, fry the meat. Fry one side for about 2 to 3 minutes, then flip and fry the other side. You may fry one piece at a time if you do not have a large pan. Use a meat thermometer to check temperature. The recommended minimum internal temperature is 145 degrees.

Drain the oil.

Place meat on a dish and garnish with dried parsley and a slice of lemon if desired. Serve with sauce.

For the sauce:
8 tablespoons unsalted butter
½ tablespoon parsley flakes

Melt the butter in a sauce pan or skillet over medium heat. Do not let it brown.

When it is melted, pour it into a bowl, or sauce boat, and sprinkle with parsley flakes.

When Abigail arrived in England, she experienced a new custom. As she wrote to her sister Mary: "You will not find at a Gentlemans table more than two dishes of meat…" She also described one such meal:

> "I returnd and dined with Mrs. Atkinson by her invitation the Evening before, in company with Mr. Smith Mrs. Hay Mr. Appleton. We had a turbot; a Soup and a roast leg of Lamb, with a cherry pye."[12]

Lamb and mutton were among the most popular meats in the eighteenth century, as modern archeologists discovered in Colonial Williamsburg.

This recipe is based on Richard Briggs' *The English Art of Cookery* (1788) and Amelia Simmons' *American Cookery* (1796). Use the top rack of the oven to roast the lamb.

Serves 4 people

6-pound leg of lamb
2-3 tablespoons softened unsalted butter
2 teaspoons salt
4 stalks of finely chopped fresh parsley leaves or 1 ¼ teaspoons dried parsley
1 tablespoon flour
lettuce leaves, for garnish
fresh parsley, for garnish
lemon slices, for garnish

Trim the meat of unnecessary fats.

Rinse the meat, then pat dry with a white paper towel.

Cover the lamb with the softened butter.

Sprinkle the salt and the parsley on the meat, then rub it in, covering the meat.

Use a colander or flour sifter to dust flour on the meat.

Seal the meat in a plastic bag. Refrigerate for 24 hours to let the meat marinate.

Set up the racks in the oven. Place a roasting pan filled with 2 cups of water on the bottom rack to catch drippings.

Preheat the oven to 475 degrees.

Remove the marinated lamb leg from the bag. Let it sit at room temperature for 15 minutes. This step is important, as it helps to keep the meat tender.

Tie the roast.

Place the lamb on the top rack and let it cook for about 20 minutes.

Reduce the temperature to 325. Let the lamb cook for another 30 minutes, checking the internal temperature until it reaches the desired level of doneness.

110 degrees: Rare
120 degrees: Medium
145 degrees: Well done.

A 6-pound leg of lamb will take about an hour to cook.

After taking the meat out of the oven, cover with aluminum foil and let it rest for 15 minutes to allow the juices to redistribute before carving the meat.

Serve on a large plate. Garnish with lettuce leaves, fresh parsley, and lemon slices.

Carving the lamb leg can be challenging. Put the knife against the shin bone and cut straight down to the end. Once you get the big piece off the leg, you can cut the other large pieces easily. After you get all the large pieces off the bone, slice the meat into smaller servings.

For the sauce:

This mint sauce is a modern interpretation of a recipe from Richard Briggs's *The English Art of Cookery* (1788).

2 tablespoons vinegar
2 tablespoons sugar
2 tablespoons water
A large handful of fresh mint leaves,
    chopped finely

Rinse mint leaves thoroughly before choppng. Mix all ingredients together in a jar. Close tightly and shake well. Refrigerate overnight. Bring to room temperature before serving.

Abigail arrived in New York on June 24, 1789, to prepare her new home at Richmond Hill as the wife of the first vice president for the new nation. On her way to New York, she spent a night in Providence, Rhode Island. She wrote of a meal there in a letter to her sister Mary.

> We proceeded to Man's Inn in Wrentham before we stop'd, 27 miles, where we dinned upon roast veal, roast chickings, salad & c. West India sweet meats I ought not to forget in the desert.[13]

Veal was a frequently consumed meat in New England, usually served stuffed. The following is based on Richard Briggs' *The English Art of Cookery* (1788) and Charlotte Mason's *The Lady's Assistant for Regulating & Supplying her Table, Being a Complete System of Cookery* (1777 edition).

6-pound shoulder veal, deboned
1 piece bread, chopped into crumbs
1 stalk rosemary, chopped fine
1 stalk savory, chopped fine
2 stalks parsley, chopped fine
4 tablespoons unsalted butter
1 teaspoon crushed black peppercorn
2 egg yolks
¼ teaspoon salt
About 1 ½ tablespoons all-purpose flour

Preheat oven 325 degrees.

Mix the bread, herbs, peppercorn, and egg yolks in a large bowl to create the stuffing,

Salt the inside the veal roast. Put the stuffing inside the veal. Seal the opening with kitchen twine.

Baste the veal with softened butter, then lightly sprinkle with flour.

Line a cookie sheet with aluminum foil. Place the veal on the sheet and cook for 20 to 25 minutes. Test the temperature with a meat thermometer. At 140 degrees, the veal will be at medium doneness.

Remove from oven and let sit for 15 minutes before carving.

John Adams wrote in his autobiography about his passage to France in May of 1778 with his son John Quincy. He described a type of soup that he had never tasted before:

> This Morning the Captain and a Passenger came on board The *Boston* from the *Julie*, a large Ship bound to Saint Domingo, to make Us a Visit. They invited Us on board to dine. Captain Palmes, Jesse Deane, John Quincy Adams and myself went, and found a very pretty Ship, an elegant Cabin and every Accomodation… The first Dish was a French soup. I had heard of Soup Meagre, which in America as well as in England had been Words of Contempt; but I thought if this was Soup Meagre, it was a very respectable thing. Then a dish of boiled Beef, as I called it, having never heard the Word Bouillie. Then the Lights of a Calf dressed one Way and the Liver another.[14]

Bouilli is a French term for boiled beef.[15] As John Adams described it, bouilli is a type of beef dish, served prior to the main course of the meal. The anonymous author of *French Domestic Cookery by an English Physician* (1825) explained that this type of soup was usually served prior to the hors d'oeuvres.

In the Early American version of bouilli, the meat would be boiled in a large pot of water, together with a variety of vegetables. The type of meat used for this recipe can vary. As the author of *French Domestic Cookery* wrote, you can add "the bones, feet, and necks of poultry or game, the meat of which has been taken for other dishes," as a way to add flavor.[16] This interpretation uses cuts of beef and beef bones.

Serves 4

  5 to 6 pints of water
  1 medium purple-top turnip
  3 medium carrots
  3 small parsnips
  1 leek
  2 medium onions
  1 pound beef stew chunks
  1 pound beef bones, cracked
  6 whole cloves
  1 ½ tablespoons salt
  Fresh parsley, chopped into garnish

Bring the water to a simmer over high heat in a heavy soup or stock pot.

Rinse the vegetables and chop them into 1-inch chunks.

Rinse the meat and the bones.

When the water simmers, turn the heat down to medium. Place the vegetables, beef and bones in the water, along with the cloves and salt.

Let the bouilli simmer slowly at medium-low heat for about 30 to 45 minutes, until the vegetables are done and the meat tender.

Discard the bones. Serve the meat and vegetables on a large plate and garnish with chopped parsley.

Photo by Ed Nute

Roast Chicken

Fowl, including game birds such as partridge, pigeon, and quail, were popular foods. Some paintings and portraits of this time, including those done by Sir Joshua Reynolds, depict young squires with packs of hounds hunting for small birds.

The Adams family also ate chicken, as indicated in the letter Abigail wrote to her sister Mary about her night in Providence.

This recipe for roast chicken is based on Richard Briggs's *The English Art of Cookery* (1788).

The illustration (see page 50) is an engraving by Boston silversmith and engraver (and patriot) Paul Revere, done for a reprinted edition, in Boston in 1772, of Susannah Carter's *The Frugal Housewife: Or, Complete Woman Cook*. His diagram shows how the skewer pins were used to pin the legs of the poultry or game bird as part of the rotisserie cooking process. For modern cooks, this recipe calls for using small skewer pins, about 4½ inches long.

Note that this recipe can be adapted for Cornish game hen, which was also popular at the time. Reduce the heat to 300 degrees and use a less butter, as the bird is smaller.

Serves 4-5

3-pound ready-to-roast chicken
2 teaspoons fresh ground pepper, divided
3 teaspoons table salt, divided
Five tablespoons unsalted butter, divided
1 tablespoon all-purpose flour, plus one pinch
Pinch of salt
2 teaspoons parsley flakes for garnish
Slices of lemon for garnish

Preheat the oven to 425 degrees.

Sprinkle the chicken's interior with 1 teaspoon of the pepper and 2 teaspoons of the salt.

Truss the chicken with skewers.

Mix 3 tablepoons butter and 1 tablespoon flour in a small bowl. Rub the mixture on the chicken. Use another tablespoon of butter to grease the roasting pan. Sprinkle a pinch of salt and a pinch of flour on the bird.

Place the bird on the greased roasting pan.

Cook the chicken for about 15 minutes, until the skin begin to turn light brown. Take the pan out of the oven and flip the bird over and spread with the remaining tablespoon of butter, a pinch of salt and a pinch of flour.

Every 10-15 minutes, take the chicken out and sprinkle with a pinch of salt and a pinch of flour.

Use a meat thermometer to check the temperature of the meat. The ideal temperature for chicken is 180 degrees. Total cooking time will be about an hour to an hour and a half.

Take the bird out and remove the skewers. Garnish with parsley flakes and lemon slices.

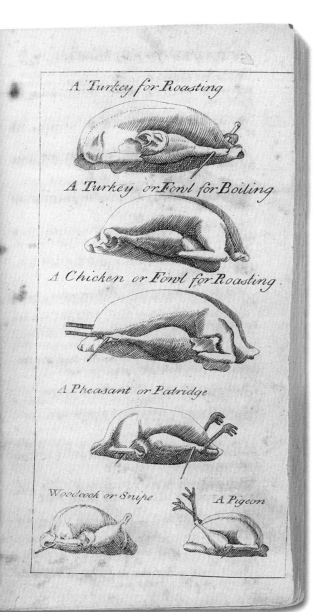

Paul Revere's engraving for a reprinted edition of Susannah Carter's cookbook *The Frugal Housewife: or, Complete woman cook*. The reprint was published in Boston in 1772. The first printing was in London, circa 1765. Notice the skewer pins are inserted at the end of the leg of a chicken. No strings are used. The diagram can be used to prepare either the Roast Chicken recipe or the Roast Turkey recipe in this cookbook. *Courtesy of Paul Revere Collection of the American Antiquarian Society.*

On December 1, 1806, John Adams sat down with his diaries and countless letters he'd written to begin penning his autobiography. In one entry on December 14, 1779, he gave an account of having turkey with M. Le Comte De Sade and "all the principal Officers of the Fleet in all the Luxury of the French Navy." He wrote:

> A very fine Turkey was brought upon Table, among every Thing else that Land, Sea or Air could furnish. One of the Captains… observed that he never saw one of these Birds on a Table but it excited in him a deep regret for the Abolition of that of Ecclesiasticks the Jesuits to whom We were he said, indebted for so many Excellent Things, and among the Rest for Turkeys. These Birds he said were never seen or known in Europe till the Jesuits imported them from India.

Adams continued by speculating on the origins of the bird.

> The French Names Dindon and poulet D'Indes, indicate that the Fowl was imported from India: But the English Name Turkey and Turkey fowl, seems to imply that the Bird was brought from the Levant. But if I am not mistaken, the English pretend that Sir Walter Raleigh first imported this Luxury from America…These important Questions of Natural History I shall leave to the Investigation and Discussion of those who have nothing else to do, nor any thing of more Taste and Consequence to contemplate.[17]

Whatever turkey's origins, it was a popular dish in John and Abigail Adamses' time.

Roasting a stuffed turkey in the eighteenth century meant keeping it over a "steady solid fire, basting frequently with butter and water," as Amelia Simmons wrote in *American Cookery*,[18] or using a reflector oven (see pages 36 and 52).

The following recipe is based on Susanna MacIver's *Cookery and Pastry* (1789 edition) and Amelia Simmons's *American Cookery* (1796). You can serve this with various side dishes. As Simmons wrote, "Serve up with boiled onions and cramberry-sauce…or celery."

1 6-pound turkey
⅓ stick of unsalted butter, plus more to butter pan
1 small loaf of wheat bread (or canned bread crumbs)
¼ cup currants
¼ cup sugar
½ teaspoon ground nutmeg
Small pieces of salt pork, finely chopped
1 stick of unsalted butter
2 egg yolks
A few sprigs of fresh parsley, chopped fine
1 tablespoon dried thyme
1 tablespoon dried summer savory
½ tablespoon fresh sweet marjoram, chopped
1 tablespoon fresh sage, chopped
½ tablespoon salt
½ tablespoon pepper
½ tablespoon flour
Curly parsley, for garnish
Apple, for garnish

If the turkey is frozen, defrost in refrigerator for 24 hours.

Preheat the oven to 450 degrees.

Line the roasting pan with aluminum foil and then grease the surface with butter.

In a large bowl, "grate a wheat loaf" and mix it with the ingredients as listed, from the currants through the pepper.
Stuff the mixture into the body cavity of the turkey. Use a piece of kitchen twine to tie the legs together.

Use skewers to pin down the wings to the body, so the turkey will stay intact as it roasts.

Abigail's kitchen at John Quincy Adams's birthplace includes a reflector oven, at the left of the fireplace, which she used for roasting any kind of meat. *Courtesy of National Park Service, Adams National Historical Park.*

Cover the bird with butter and flour.

Set the bird on the roasting pan with breast side up.

Put in the oven and roast for about 3 to 3½ hours. The internal temperature should read 170 degrees.

Garnish with parsley on the side, with an apple placed in the parsley.

This recipe for gravy is based on Susanna MacIver's *Cookery and Pastry* (1789 edition), which reads:

Make a sauce of some thin sliced bread, some water, a little white wine, a blade of mace, some sugar, and a piece of fresh butter; let all boil until it is very smooth, and do not let it be too thick. Send it up in a sauce-boat.

1 or 2 slices wheat bread
1 ½ cups water
¼ cup sweet white wine (i.e. Rhine)
½ teaspoon ground mace
3 tablespoons sugar
1 tablespoon unsalted butter

In a sauce pan, boil the bread pieces with water and the other ingredients listed.

Roast Duck Stuffed with Sliced Onions

On September 7, 1774, John Adams wrote in his diary:

> Dined with Mr. Miers Fisher, a young Quaker and a Lawyer. We saw his Library, which is clever. But this plain Friend, and his plain, tho pretty Wife, with her Thee's and Thou's, had provided us the most Costly Entertainment—Ducks, Hams, Chickens, Beef, Pigg, Tarts, Creams, Custards, Gellies, fools, Trifles, floating Islands, Beer, Porter, Punch, Wine and a long &c.19

This recipe is an example of what John Adams might have eaten at this young Quaker's elegant home. It is based on John Perkins' *Every Woman Her Own House-Keeper; Or The Ladies' Library* (1796).

If you can't find fresh duck, frozen duck is an option. Ducks are often available at Chinese supermarkets. Check the freshness by making sure the color of the bird is pale white, not dark pink.

If the duck is frozen, be sure to thaw it in a bowl of water or the refrigerator for a day, according to USDA guidelines.

Photo by Ed Nute

Also, remember that the size of the bird will influence the cooking time, as will the type of oven you use.

Serves 4-5 people

  4.75-5 pounds fresh ready-to-cook duck
  1 stick unsalted butter, divided and softened
  ½ teaspoon pepper
  1 teaspoon salt
  Leaves from about 3 stalks fresh sage, chopped, or 2 teaspoons dried sage
  1 medium size onion, sliced
  1½ tablespoons all-purpose flour
  Sliced lemons for garnish

Preheat the oven to 300 degrees.

If using a fresh duck, clean the bird and remove any giblets. If the duck is frozen, defrost in refrigerator for 24 hours.

Chop off the duck's feet by cutting them at the first joint. Chop off the neck. Remove the wishbone to make the duck easy to carve after it is cooked.

Wash the duck, then dry with a white paper towel.

In a small mixing bowl, mix 2 tablespoon of the butter with the pepper, salt, and sage.

Rub the butter mixture inside the bird. Then stuff the bird with the sliced onion.

Butter the roasting pan with 1 tablespoon of the butter.

Use skewer pins to close the end of the bird, inserting the pins through the lower part of the legs. Use skewer pins to keep the wings attached to the breast.

Place the duck breast-side up on the roasting pan. Cover the duck with 2 tablespoons butter then dust lightly with flour.

Place the pan on the center rack of the oven. Cook the duck for 15 minutes until the skin is light brown

Take the pan out to remarinate the bird with the remaining butter, using a knife to spread the butter on the skin. Lightly sprinkle more flour on the skin. Put it back into the oven and turn down the temperature to 350 degrees.

Let it cook for about 30 minutes. Take the duck out of the oven and flip the bird over to allow the other side to cook for about 10 minutes.

Take it out and flip it back to the breast-side-up. Cook for 10 to 15 minutes.

Cook until a meat thermometer shows the internal temperature is 165 degrees. The juice should be light yellow with no bloody discharge. The skin should be medium brown.

Place the duck on a large plate. Garnish with sliced lemons.

Photo by Ed Nute

CHAPTER 4

Sauces

Early in his marriage, John Adams wrote about his family's visits to the home of Abigail's uncle Dr. Cotton Tufts. Abigail's sister Mary Smith Cranch, and her family, would visit at the same time.

> Arrived at Dr. Tufts's, where I found a fine Wild Goose on the Spit and Cramberries stewing in the Skillet for Dinner. Tufts as soon as he heard that Cranch was at Braintree determined to go over, and bring him and Wife and Child and my Wife and Child over to dine upon wild Goose and Cramberry Sause.[1]

A recipe for cranberry sauce appeared in the first cookbook by an American author, Amelia Simmons's *American Cookery*. She suggested that roasted turkey be served with "cramberry-sauce." This idea went back to medieval English cookery, when barberries were eaten as a side meat and poultry dishes.[2]

In 1821, William Tudor, a local Boston author and the cofounder of *North American Review*, published a collection of memoirs titled *Miscellaneous*, which included an essay on cranberry sauce. Critiquing simple American lives, which foreign nations would view as "barbarous," Tudor included instructions on how cranberry sauce was prepared:

> The berries are stewed slowly with nearly the weight of sugar for about an hour, and served on the table cold: the sugar made use of differs in quality according to the wealth of those by whom the sauce is used.[3]

For this modern interpretation, you may use granulated sugar, brown sugar, or molasses.

   1 12-ounce bag of fresh cranberries, washed
   1 cup water
   6 tablespoons brown sugar

Rinse the cranberries.

In a cast-iron skillet, place the cranberries in a cup of water and stew them at medium heat.

When you start hearing and seeing the cranberries break apart, slowly stir with a spoon and add sugar, mixing well, to taste.

When the mixture cools, refrigerate, and then serve cold.

While visiting friends in Boston, Abigail Adams wrote to her husband on August 22, 1777, about a certain type of sauce. She frequently kept her husband up to date about their household affairs at the farm. This time she wrote, "We are like to have a plenty of sause. I shall fat Beaf and pork enough, make butter and cheese enough. If I have neither Sugar, molasses, coffe nor Tea."[4]

The type of sauce to which she was referring was garden sauce, frequently used for any type of meat dish. It is also known as green sauce in the Oxford English Dictionary. The following recipe is based on Hannah Woolley's *The Compleat Servant-maid; Or, The Young Maidens Tutor*, published in 1677.

¼ cup water
½ cup white vinegar
2 ½ tablespoons sugar
2 or 3 large pieces of sorrel, finely chopped
½ piece white bread
½ of a sweet apple, cored and pared

In a sauce pan, boil the water, white vinegar and sugar.

As the mixture boils, add the sorrel, white bread, and the apple. You can use day-old bread for this recipe. Add some water if it sticks to the pan. Slowly boil until the apple softens and the bread turns into mush.

Store in sealed containers or glass jars.

Photo by Ed Nute

CHAPTER 5

Seafood

Traditional New England cuisine would include some sort of seafood, especially for those who lived near the ocean or a harbor. North Atlantic fish and crustaceans included cod, haddock, salmon, and lobster. As an envoy to France, John Adams discussed fishing laws in his native New England. He was concerned that the activities of the British navy would harm fishing, whaling, and lobstering commerce.

Selecting good seafood in the eighteenth century was similar to choosing good food today. The golden rule on buying fish can be found in *Cookery Reformed: Or, the Lady's Assistant* (1755): "The freshness of fish is generally known by the gills and the eyes." Avoid fish with "their eyes faded, sunk and wrinkled."[80]

Fish and tender meats were cooked with a game bird roaster, rather than a reflector oven. A gridiron could be used to broil fish.

In late July of 1784, after arriving in London, Abigail Adams began to adapt to her new European lifestyle as a diplomat's wife. She recorded the names of guests she received throughout each day. Receiving illustrious visitors was one of many novel experiences for this modest New England woman.

One of her visitors was the American expatriate Michael Joy. Joy was a son of a loyalist who had fled Boston in 1776. Once settled in London, he found work in shipping and trade. He had encountered John Adams in Passy, France, a few years before meeting Abigail. Despite his loyalty to the British, he ultimately became a member of the Massachusetts Historical Society in 1816. After a dinner one evening with Mr. Joy, Abigail wrote to her sister:

> Our dinner consisted of fried fish of a small kind, a boiled ham, a fillet of veal, and a pair of roast ducks, and almond pudding, currants and gooseberries, which in this country are very fine.[2]

One of Abigail's contemporaries, Susannah Carter, presented a similar recipe for fried fish in her work *The Frugal Housewife: Or, Complete Woman Cook* (1796 edition). Carter wrote, "Small fish are generally dressed to garnish a dish of fish, as smelts, gudgeons, roach, small whitings &c."[3]

The process of frying fish has not changed much since Abigail's time, with the exception of using vegetable- or nut-based oils for frying instead of less healthy lard or animal fats. This modern interpretation also calls for fresh parsley, rather than dried.

You can find precleaned smelts and whitings at seafood markets. They are relatively inexpensive. Asking the sales person to gut the fish and remove the heads will reduce the preparation time significantly. If purchasing frozen fish, be sure to defrost them properly to avoid any food-borne diseases.

Photo by Ed Nute

Serves 3 to 4 people

    1 pound smelts and 1 pound whitings, cleaned and gutted, without heads
    2 egg yolks
    ¼ cup flour
    1 cup canola oil
    Parsley flakes, or fresh parsley
    A few slices of lemon

Rinse the fish, then pat dry with a white paper towel.

Remove bones from whitings if desired: Use a small sharp knife to make an incision on the belly. Then, slip the thumb under the spine and slowly peel away the long back bone.

Beat the egg yolks. Spread them over the fish using a pastry brush.

Sprinkle the flour over the fish.

Fry evenly in a large nonstick pan with 1 cup of canola oil. Keep the heat at medium level to avoid burning the fish.

Spread fish on absorbent paper towels, then plate and garnish with parsley and lemon.

If you'd like, try frying the parsley. Do so after you have fried the fish and be careful not to burn the plant.

Susannah Carter wrote, "As these sorts of fish are generally dressed by themselves, for supper, you may send various sauces, as you like best." She recommended several kinds of sauces, including shrimp sauce. Although Abigail did not mention having shrimp sauce with her fried fish, this type of anchovy sauce was an option at that time. This recipe is based on Carter's *The Frugal Housewife: Or, Complete Woman Cook* (1796 edition).

  1-2 cooked anchovies, or 4 from a can
  1 cup water
  1 tablespoon margarine
  1 teaspoon pepper
  ¼ teaspoon red wine
  ¼ teaspoon salt, or to taste
  1 teaspoon lemon juice
  2 teaspoons all-purpose flour

Boil the anchovies in a small sauce pan in the cup of water for about 15 minutes. If using anchovies from a can, soak them in a bowl of cold water for an hour first to get rid of the sodium.

Smash the anchovies until the fish is in fine pieces. Use a seive to separate the meat from the liquid. Set both aside.

Pour the anchovy liquid into another small pan. As it starts to boil, add the margarine and stir until it melts. Add the pepper and the wine, and stir.

Add the lemon juice, and stir.

While quickly stirring, shake in the flour to thicken the sauce. Stir.

In the eighteenth-century, oysters were a popular snack and were also served for breakfast. In many seaports like London and Boston, oysters could be easily caught and sold. Young women or street traders carried baskets of them crying out "Oysters!" or singing songs about oysters to drum up business.

In his travels in the colonies and abroad, John Adams witnessed many different types of oysters. In his diary entry on September 11, 1774, John was in Philadelphia and wrote this:

> By Mr. Peters, written at the Bar and given to a Judge Mr. Willing, who had asked the Question at Dinner, in Pleasantry. Mr. Willing is the most sociable, agreeable Man of all. He told us of a Law of this Place, that whereas oysters, between the Months of May and Septr. were found to be unwholesome food, if any were brought to Market they should be forfeited and given to the Poor.

Early in their courtship, John Adams had written to Abigail about his smallpox inoculation. (Cotton Mather had introduced the practice before Adams was born, adapting a procedure he learned from one of his slaves from West Africa. While the inoculation was controversial at first, by the time Adams became an adult, the practice became common. A small amount of cow pox was inserted into a patient's skin. In April of 1764, John went to Boston to receive the treatment.)

His doctors suggested that he eat something light, and he wrote to Abigail: "I drank Frontinac and Mountain Malaga, and eat Oysters in order to make the Pock fill well, till I filled up about 30 fine ones."[4]

Notable Bostonian silversmith and engraver Paul Revere published political prints, including his famous interpretation of the Boston Massacre. John Adams defended the British soldiers who had fired on the crowd, noting in his argument that the soldiers had suffered assault themselves in the form of "every snow-ball, oyster shell, cake of ice, or bit of cinder that was thrown that night." *The Boston Massacre.* Engraving by Paul Revere. *Courtesy of Massachusetts Archives, AR22/ A084, Paul Revere Engraving Plates, Boston Massacre.*

Oysters even played a role in the famous Boston Massacre of March 5, 1770. Because he believed that all men were entitled to a fair trial, John defended the British soldiers who had fired on the crowd, killing five Bostonians, arguing that their actions were an act of self-defense. In John's argument for their defense, he wrote:

> Every snow-ball, oyster shell, cake of ice, or bit of cinder that was thrown that night, at the Sentinel, was an assault upon him; every one that was thrown at the party of soldiers, was an assault upon them, whether it hit any of them or not. I am guilty of an assault, if I present a gun at any person, whether I shoot at him or not, it is an assault, and if I insult him in that manner, and he shoots me, it is but manslaughter.[5]

Six of the soldiers were acquitted by the jury and two were found guilty of manslaughter, but not murder, and so were not put to death.

Years later, as he sat down to write his autobiography, the elder statesman reflected on different places he traveled in Europe. In December of 1779, he and his sons John Quincy and Charles visited El Ferrol in Spain when their ship stopped there due to damages from the transatlantic journey. Based on the journal entries he had written more than four decades earlier, John particularly remembered:

> The Bread, the Cabbages, Colliflowers, Apples, Pears &c. are good. The Beef, Pork, Poultry &c. are good. The Fish are good, excellent Eels, Sardines and other fish and tolerable Oysters, but not like ours.[6]

As President, John Adams occasionally enjoyed oysters. In a letter to Abigail, he wrote:

> From Rileys in Berlin, We went to Newhaven 26 miles to dinner at your Friends Mrs. Smiths who were very respectfully inquisitive after your health, and very sorry to hear an Account of it from me, not so flattering. A Visit from Dr. Dwight detained Us agreably for a short time but We found enough to cross the Ferry over the Housatonnoc by sunsett and soon reached Lovejoys in this Town. We had our Fire made in our Bedchamber and our Tea and Oysters Served up.[7]

Here is a modern interpretation of Susannah Carter's recipe for oysters in *The Frugal Housewife: Or, Complete Woman Cook* (1796 edition).

1 egg, beaten
2 tablespoons milk
1 teaspoon ground mace
½ tablespoon flour
A dozen raw oysters, cleaned, removed from shells
⅓ cup bread crumbs
5 tablespoons unsalted butter, or cooking oil for frying

In a bowl, mix the egg, milk and mace. Add the flour slowly, continuing to mix.

Dip the oysters in the mixture. Put bread crumbs on a plate. Coat the dipped oysters with the bread crumbs.

In a nonstick frying pan or a cast-iron skillet, melt the butter or heat the cooking oil. When the skillet is hot, slowly put the oysters in the fat, and fry them until light golden brown.

Remove the oysters from the pan, and serve.

On January 16, 1797, about two weeks after winning the presidential election, John Adams wrote to Abigail about his mixed feelings over the election results. Because the Federalist fraction won the race, there were concerns on the part of the Republicans or French sympathizers. The French people in the new nation, he wrote, "seem to be disappointed and a little bit confounded."[8]

Despite inheriting issues of strained relationships with France and witnessing political divisions within his new country, Adams briefly enjoyed this victory by exchanging with Abigail a "List of the best natured Toasts" he ever read. He said:

> They were sent me in a Baltimore Paper. They are peculiarly indulgent to me, as they allow me, Salmon and Lobster in Addition to Hay, Homminy, Mush, Milk and Cider. There is no Malice in any of them.[9]

This salmon dish was served during John and Abigail's time. To make it easier for shoppers, the modern version calls for salmon fillet rather than a whole fish. Both *The Practice of Cookery and Pastry* (1791) and *The Complete Family-Piece* (1737) give examples of this typical dish. The salmon can be served with oyster sauce.

Serves 3-4

    1 whole salmon fillet (usually about 2.5 pounds)
    Olive oil or unsalted butter
    ½ teaspoon ground nutmeg
    ½ teaspoon ground cinnamon
    ½ teaspoon ground allspice
    Fresh parsley, chopped
    Few pinches of salt or freshly ground salt
    Small amount of grated bread crumbs from wheat bread or dark rye bread

Preheat the oven to 300 degrees.

Wash the fish, and remove the scales. You can get the butcher to do this for you.

Put olive oil or melted, unsalted butter on a sheet pan.

Mix the ground spices together.

Sprinkle some of the mixture on both sides of the fish.

Sprinkle chopped parsley on the fish. Then sprinkle salt on the fish. Finally, sprinkle the fish with the bread crumbs.

Place the fish in the oven. Cook for about 10 to 13 minutes.

Serve fish on a large plate and garnish with more fresh parsley, if desired.

10 raw oysters and their liquids, removed from their shells
¼ cup of water (optional)
2 tablespoons unsalted butter
¼ teaspoon ground nutmeg
3 tablespoons white wine
3 tablespoons half and half
½ teaspoon all-purpose flour

Remove oysters from the shells, and reserve the liquids. Clean the oysters.

Place the liquids and the oysters in a bowl. Keep a quarter cup of water nearby for the next step. When cooking, if the mixture becomes too dry, add water.

In a small sauce pan, slowly melt the butter.

Add the nutmeg, white wine and the half and half. Then add the oysters and the liquids into the mixture. Stir slowly, with the heat on low. It should be steaming, but do not overboil.

Slowly sprinkle in the flour to thicken the mixture.

Serve in a sauce bowl.

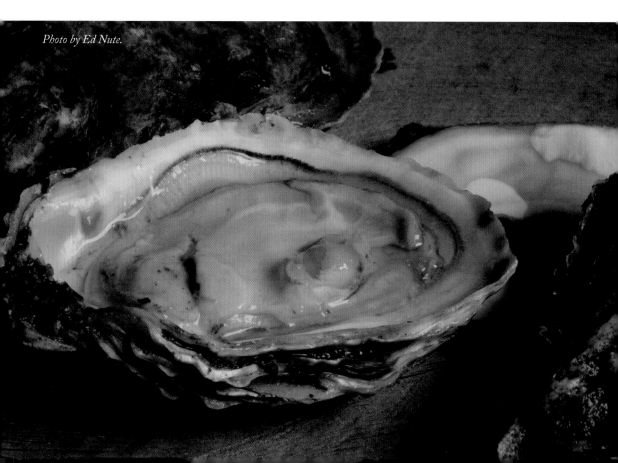

Photo by Ed Nute.

Baked Salmon Fillet

During one of John Adams's darkest months in Europe, he received a letter from Abigail trying to lift his spirits. He was in France working out details of the American treaty with England and working on negotiations among Spain, France, and England.

Chinese exports, including this fish platter with divider, were purchased abroad. This platter was frequently used by John and Abigail Adams for dishes with a juice. *Courtesy of National Park Service, Adams National Historical Park.*

> I would give you a fine Salmon, a pair of roast Brants and a custard, can you dine upon such a Slender number of dishes after having been accustomed to 50 and a hundred. Aya but say you true Friendship, tender affection and mutual Love are to be found there, and that is a feast I meet not with abroad. Come then and join in the Feast of reason and flow of Soul. Come and give happiness to her who know not either solid pleasure or real felicity seperated from you...[10]

The following recipe is based on one from Hannah Glasse's *The Art of Cookery Made Plain and Easy* (1784 edition).

1 large fillet of salmon (1-2 pounds)
¼ teaspoon ground cloves
¾ teaspoons ground nutmeg
¾ teaspoon ground coriander seeds
¾ teaspoon salt
¾ teaspoon ground pepper
1 egg
¼ cup 1% milk
1 slice wheat or multigrain bread, finely chopped or 1 tablespoon prepared breadcrumbs
Lemon, sliced, for garnish
Fresh parsley for garnish

Preheat the oven to 350 degrees.

Wash the fillet and then dry with a white paper towel.

In a small mixing bowl, mix all the spices. Sprinkle them on the fillet.

In another mixing bowl, mix the egg, milk and bread (or breadcrumbs). Spread the mixture on the fillet.

Place the salmon fillet on aluminum foil with the scale-side down. Seal tightly with another piece of aluminum foil. Bake for about 30 minutes. The fish should flake easily and should retain some its juice.

Serve on a plate with lemon and parsley as garnish.

This is another way to make salmon, based on two works, *John Farley's The London Art of Cookery* (1811 edition), and *Cookery Reformed: Or, the Lady's Assistant* (1755).

- 1 whole salmon fillet, scales removed
- Olive oil or melted unsalted butter
- 1 tablespoon flour
- 1 tablespoon ground black pepper
- 1 tablespoon salt
- Lemon, sliced, for garnish
- Fresh parsley for garnish

Preheat oven to 300 degrees.

Wash the fillet and then dry it with a white paper towel.

Dip the fillet in olive oil or melted unsalted butter.

Cut the fillet into strips 2 inches wide.

Sprinkle flour on the pieces of salmon.

Place the fish on a broiler pan. Lightly sprinkle it with pepper and salt.

Place the fish in the oven and cook about five minutes. Flip the fish once to let the other side cook for a few minutes. Flip it again to let it cook for an additional minute or two.

Serve with lemon slices and fresh parsley and a sauce of more melted butter, if desired.

In October of 1789, Abigail Adams wrote from Richmond Hill, their temporary home in New York, to John Adams, explaining how she sent cod to one of their friends who would later become the first chief justice of the Supreme Court.

> I have received the fish in four Boxes and tried some of it, which proves very fine, One Box I have sent to Mr. [John] Jay as a present from You.[11]

Cod has a rich history in Massachusetts. A little more than a hundred years before John and Abigail Adams were born, Bartholomew Gosnold led a European expedition to the Cape, which he called Shoal Hope. His men, though, insisted on calling the area Cape Cod because of the abundance of the fish.[12] In June of 1783, nearly a year after the Treaty of Paris was signed, John's brother-in-law, Richard Cranch reported that the fishermen of Massachusetts were pleased with news of John's success in securing rights for the North Atlantic cod fisheries.

> I have also been favour'd with the sight of several of your other Letters, particularly one to Uncle Smith about the Fishery; and I got liberty from him to let some of your Essex Friends have a sight of it … and some other Members of the Fishing Towns… An unrestrained Fishery obtained…All these and a thousand other publick Benefits, we think ourselves indebted for, to your Virtue, great Abilities and indefatigable Application in favour of your Country.[13]

In September of that year, John Adams replied:

> If my Townsmen of Marblehead, Salem, Cape Anne, Plymouth &c. are pleased with the Peace, I am very glad: But We have yet to Secure, if We can, the Right to carry Some of their Fish to market.[14]

This recipe serves as a tribute to John Adams's work fighting for the rights of fishermen in Massachusetts. Try it with Sarah Harrison's fish sauce, on page 72.

Serves 3-4 people

cod fillet
1 teaspoon salt
lemon slices
parsley flakes
horseradish

Cut the fillet into pieces about 5 or 6 inches long.

Put the fillet in a saucepan or frying pan and cover with water. Add the salt.

Boil the fish at medium heat for about 10 minutes. Check the fish often. The cooked fish should be flaky.

Carefully remove fish (which will be fragile) from water.

Garnish with lemon slices and parsley and serve horseradish on the side.

For the fish sauce:

This is a modern interpretation of Sarah Harrison's "Sauce for Fish," from *The House-Keeper's Pocket-Book* (1739). Harrison's recipe calls for "a few sprigs of sweet herbs." The herbs listed here are based on what Abigail Adams grew in her working garden at Peace field.

1 shallot
1 slice lemon
1 cup water
½ cup claret
1 teaspoon black pepper
1 teaspoon savory (dried or fresh)
1 teaspoon basil
1 teaspoon sage
1 teaspoon ground mace
2 anchovies (canned, or fresh and deboned with an additional 1 teaspoon of salt)
1 pinch black pepper
2 tablespoons butter
1 teaspoon finely shredded horseradish (optional)

Mix all the ingredients in a sauce pan. Boil for 30 minutes until the anchovy breaks up into the sauce. Use a colander to strain the sauce. Serve along with any fish dish.

On December 15, 1782, John Adams wrote to his close friend and brother-in-law Richard Cranch about negotiations that would eventually lead to the Treaty of Paris.

> Since my Arrival here 26 October, until the 30 of November, We had a constant Scuffle Morning noon and night about Cod and Haddock on the Grand Bank Deer skins on the Ohio and Pine Trees at Penobscat, and...all the Refugees.[15]

In 1783, when the treaty was signed, Adams had a seal made to commemorate the occasion. The seal included images of a deer, a pine tree, and a swimming fish.[16]

The following recipe is a modern interpretation of one from John Conrade Cooke's *Cookery and Confectionary*, 1824, which said to:

> Take the filet off the bone; dip them in egg and bread crumbs; fry in hot lard: or they may be fried whole the same way; serve lobster (no.87) oyster (no.93) or anchovy sauce.

1 pound haddock fillet
½ tablespoon salt
1 egg
1 ½ tablespoons breadcrumbs
2 tablespoons unsalted butter or cooking oil

Remove any scales from the fish, then rinse it and pat dry with a paper towel.

Sprinkle salt on both sides.

In a bowl, whisk the egg with the breadcrumbs until the mixture thickens.
Spread the mixture onto the fillet.

In a large frying skillet, melt the butter or heat the cooking oil. Fry the fish for 7 to 10 minutes on each side until it is a light, golden brown.

In the eighteenth century, an iron rod was speared through a lobster, and then the lobster was roasted over an open fire. Or, the lobster was put in a dish in front of the fire and basted with butter. The following recipe is based on Hannah Glasse's *The Art of Cookery Made Plain and Easy* (1784 edition) and Richard Briggs's *The English Art of Cookery* (1788).

    3 small, or chicken, lobsters (up to 1.25 pounds each)
    8 tablespoons unsalted butter

Preheat oven to 425 degrees.

Cover a baking sheet with aluminum foil. Set aside.

Boil the lobsters for about 15 to 20 minutes, until they are about three-quarters cooked.

Melt the butter in a sauce pan. Don't let it burn. Pour it into a bowl.

Separate the lobsters' heads and tails. Slice the tails in half. Crack the claws.

Baste the lobster parts with melted butter and place on baking sheet. Cook for 10 to 15 minutes. The internal temperature of the meat should reach 145 degrees.

Serve with the rest of the melted butter.

Boiled lobster

In the Adamses' time, lobster served as food for slaves and livestock and was used for fertilizer for the farm. Although John and Abigail hardly mentioned lobster in their letters, during the Revolutionary War, the word "lobster" was frequently used to refer to the British soldiers who fired at the crowd in the streets of Boston during the Boston Massacre. It was not only because the soldiers wore bright red coats, but also because the term meant a "a fool or a dupe."[17]

Serves 3-4

3 medium lobsters (about 1.5 pounds each)
Butter
Lemon slices

Boil water in a large pot. For each lobster, you'll need about 3 quarts of water. Place lobsters in pot. Boil for about 20 to 25 minutes until the meat is tender and the shell turns bright red orange. Cooking times will vary with the size of the lobsters.

Serve with melted butter and lemon slices.

Photo by Ed Nute

Photo by Ed Nute

CHAPTER 6

Vegetables

While vegetables were not the major portion of New Englanders' diets in the eighteenth century because the environment posed a challenge to growing them, vegetables and gardening were an essential part of the Adamses' daily life—and something they enjoyed. John frequently observed the practices of other farmers. In 1795, he wrote:

> It would give me great Pleasure, to visit General Gates and make my Observations on his Husbandry and Gardening: I should hope to learn Lessons and acquire Experience in my favourite Business and Amusement.[1]

Additionally, the Adamses sometimes bought fresh vegetables at local markets in cities.

Recalling his travels in Europe, John Adams once recorded the abundance of vegetables in a market that he visited in Astorga, Spain, in January of 1780.

> Saw the Market of Vegetables. The Onions and Turnips were the largest and finest I ever saw. The Cabbages, Carrots &c. appeared very good…the Marragatto Women attended the Market with their Vendibles. These were as fine as any of our American Indian Squaw…[2]

Earlier, in October of 1783, in France, John settled at his new residence in Auteuil, and wrote to Abigail about the garden.

> There is a large Garden, full of all Vegetables and Fruits as Grapes, Pears, Peaches. There is besides a large Flower Garden….It is full of Flowers and of Roots and Vegetables of all Kinds, and of Fruits. Grapes of several sorts and of excellent Quality. Pears, Peaches &c. But every Thing suffers for want of Manure. There is an Acre or two of Ground, without the Garden Fence which belongs to the Estate, which affords Pasture for a Cow, but the Land is poor.[3]

When Abigail went to London, she compared the vegetables for sale with the ones back in Massachusetts. In a letter to Isaac Smith, Sr., in May 8, 1785, she reported, "Vegetables and fruit are not so high as in London, but all enormus when compared to Boston Market."[4]

While Abigail found London to be busy and densely populated, she also found resemblances to Boston: In a letter to her sister Mary, dated September 12, 1786, she wrote: "The Country is exceeding fruitfull and every house has a Garden Spot, plentifully stored with vegetables."[5]

When they returned to the United States and moved into their new home, later named Peace field, the Adamses continued to farm and grew a variety of vegetables and fruits. The majority of them were cash crops sold at local markets, but some were for personal consumption.

When he became vice president of the United States, John took up residence at Richmond Hill, a home just outside of the temporary capital in New York, in what is now the heart of Greenwich Village in Manhattan. In May of 1789, he reported to his wife on the garden:

> I have taken an House, and now wish you to come on, as soon as possible. It will be necessary to Send by Water all the Carpets that are not in Use, and Several Beds, Bedsteads, Bedding Bed and Table Linnen, —Plate China &c. if you can convey it to Providence would come better that Way. The House is on the North River about a mile out of the City, in a fine situation, a good Stable, Coach House, Garden, about 30 Acres of Land. It goes by the name of Mr. Montiere House. We may keep two Cows, on the Pasture.[102]

At Richmond Hill, Abigail Adams made the home comfortable for her husband and the family, overseeing the servants who did the majority of the cooking. As a way to keep the family's expenses low, she sometimes purchased vegetables from local people, including General Horatio Gates. In a letter to John, she reported:

> I went on tuesday to Breakfast at Rose Hill, General [Horatio] Gates Seat. I am solisitious You should see it. It is the most Beautifull Spot I have seen here, 92 acres of Excellent land, and a House to gratify any moderate ambition for two thousand pounds, was a bargain indeed tho only a Life estate. I walk with the General to his Garden, to his Farm house, and to his Barns, to his Feilds of Grain &c. He may literally be said to live in clover. He pointed to a parsnip bed in his garden perhaps a quarter of an Acre, and told me that he made 27 pounds from that spot the last Year beside sufficint for his Family and this Year says he from that Spinnage bed about about 20 foot, I have taken 20 pounds, and my Sparigrass beds neated 3 pounds per day during the Season of it. The Market people go to the Garden and take it so that he has no trouble of sending it to Market...[7]

As the vice president's wife, Abigail sometimes preferred to have vegetables sent from Boston, due to the high cost of produce in New York: "It really would have been worth while to have brought our vegetables in Boston. Potatoes particularly for they are at 9 shilling a Bushel by the Quantity, turnips at 1/6."[8]

When the capital moved to Philadelphia, the Adamses relocated to Bush Hill, which was once a home belonging to Scottish lawyer William Hamilton. Here, too, Abigail said she had problems with inflated food prices. She complained to John:

> The whole Garden is not so large as our lower Garden, but vegitables are very dear in the market, cowcumbers sold at 3 shillings a peice a fort night ago. Mr. Hammond has a Garden out below where we used to live at Greenwich. He told me one day last week that his Gardener sold in one day 60 dollars worth of vegitables. When shall we Farm so?[9]

Although John and Abigail Adams did not keep a separate diary about farming and gardening as did some of their contemporaries, their famous correspondence has many references to farming practices. John often advised her on keeping up the family farm while he was in New York and Philadelphia.

In March of 1794, John instructed Abigail:

> Plant the Ground which broke up last fall with corn. Sow Barley, where We had corn last Year. Plant again the lower Garden. Potatoes again at the Beach Meadow. Plant again Farons last Years Corn field. Buy as many Cows and young Stock as you can keep in plenty. Send the sheep as soon as convenient to the Pasture by Harmans.[10]

As John Adams' tenure in office came to a close, Abigail reminded him to look forward to spending time at his beloved farm:

> I hope the time is not far distant when you may return to the Rural amusements of you, farm snatch a comfort from its opening verduer, and forget the labours and toils of the State, amidst the blooming orchard and the springing blade.[11]

This chapter focuses on some of the vegetables the Adamses enjoyed in their lives. One note: Vegetables in those days tended to be almost fully cooked, except for salads. People did not understand that if they overcooked the vegetables it would lower the nutritional value. Most vegetables were boiled along with salted meats.

Some cookbook authors like Hannah Glasse were ahead of their time and warned about overboiling the vegetables. In *The Art of Cookery Made Plain and Easy* (1784 edition), she wrote:

> Most people spoil garden things by over boiling them. All things that are green should have a little crispness, for if they are over-boiled they neither have any sweetness or beauty.

A note on herbs

In the eighteenth century, herbs were used for cooking and as home remedies. John recorded in his diary some of the herbs he used to treat his own discomforts.

> I took Rhubarb and Salt of Wormwood… Bathing my Feet and drinking balm Tea, last night composed me somewhat, and I hope the Rhubarb and Salt of Wormwood I took this Morning will carry off my Complaints.[12]

Herbs served as "domestic medicine," as John Duffy wrote in his work *From Humors to Medical Science: A History of American Medicine.*[13]

Many cookbooks of the era included sections on home remedies. Housewives like Abigail Adams were taught to be familiar with herbs and their usages and learned how to preserve them.

As the First Lady, Abigail recommended that her husband treat his cough in October of 1799: "get some oxemal squills, and take two Teaspoon full in any tea drink of Hysop or Sage, or Balm" before going to bed.[14]

In her letters, Abigail frequently mentioned herbs including sage, mint, catnip, calmol, hyssop, tansey, and wormwood. (Note that tansey is highly toxic while other herbs, such as wormwood and hyssop can be dangerous if consumed in high quantities.)

Few surviving eighteenth-century homes still have their gardens. In museum homes such as the Paul Revere House in the North End of Boston, curators often create a reproduction of the type of garden that a family would have had. Revere, for example, probably would have had herbs, herbal flowers, and maybe a pear tree.

John and Abigail's garden at Peace field was not as elegant as the formal English garden that exists there today for visitors. In their time, the garden was a lot smaller. It was a working

Photo by Ed Nute

garden, where they grew vegetables for their own consumption. While John would tend the corn stalks, Abigail tended the flowers, vegetables, and herbs in her kitchen garden.

When John was away from home, he frequently thought of walking in the garden with his children and his "dearest friend." In a letter to Abigail, he wrote:

> My Refreshment is a flight to [Braintree] …takes a Walk with you, and your little prattling, Nabby, Johnny, Charly, and Tommy. We walk all together up Penn's Hill, over the Bridge to the Plain, down to the Garden, &c.[15]

In 1789, Abigail Adams wrote to John Adams from Peace field, their new home in what is now Quincy, Massachusetts.

> My Garden looks charmingly but it wants warmth. I have got some large asparagrass Bed made, and my little grass plots before the door, pay well for the manure which I had put on.[16]

This recipe is based on one found in Amelia Simmons' *American Cookery* (1796).

    1 bunch asparagus
    2 tablespoons unsalted butter
    water
    1 tablespoon salt
    2 tablespoons cooking oil
    2 tablespoons unsalted butter
    1 slice of toasted white or wheat bread
    3 small slices of an orange, for garnish

Wash the asparagus, cut off the lower ends (white part), and then cut the stalks in half.

In a small saucepan or frying pan, melt the butter, swirling it over medium heat (do not let it brown).

Fill another saucepan with about 4 cups water. As it begins to boil, add salt and cooking oil. Add the asparagus and cook at a high simmer for about 3 minutes. Remove asparagus with a strainer, set aside both the water and the asapargus..

Dip the toasted bread in the water, then place on the bottom of a dish. Place the asparagus on top. Pour the melted butter on the asparagus.

Serve with buttery egg sauce on the side.

For the egg sauce:
    2 boiled eggs
    3 tablespoons unsalted butter
    ½ teaspoon nutmeg
    ¼ teaspoon salt
    1 teaspoon vinegar

Peel the shells off the boiled eggs, then chop the eggs finely. Place in a bowl.

Melt the butter in a frying pan over medium heat. Swirl the butter around the pan to melt it evenly.

Pour the melted butter into the eggs, while stirring. Add the nutmeg, salt, and vinegar. Stir until the mixture looks creamy. (If you need more melted butter, you may make some more.)

Pour sauce, as desired, over the asparagus.

John Adams wrote to Abigail Adams on July 9, 1774, at Falmouth, to describe one of his many "genteel" dinners.

> Saturday I dined with him [Coddman] in Company with Brigadier Prebble, Major Freeman and his son, &c. and very genteel Dinner we had. Salt Fish and all its apparatus, roast Chickens, Bacon, Pees, as fine a Salad as ever was made, and a rich meat Pie-Tarts and Custards &c., good Wine and as good Punch as ever you made.[17]

For this recipe, based on Amelia Simmons's *American Cookery* (1796), you can use frozen peas.

1 16-ounce bag of green peas
1 tablespoon sugar
1 teaspoon salt
1 tablespoon unsalted butter
1 stalk mint, chopped

Bring a cup of water to a boil in a pan. Add the peas, as well as the sugar and salt. Boil for about 7 minutes.

Strain peas in a colander. Place them in a serving dish and stir in the butter. Garnish with mint.

In a letter to Abigail Adams, John wrote, "Digging in a Potato Yard upon my own Garden and living in my own Family would be to me Paradise."[18]

Potatoes were a staple in the Colonial diet, as they were relatively easy to grow in the harsh climate. As Amelia Simmons wrote in *American Cookery* in 1796, potatoes "rank for universal use, profit and easy acquirement."

Based on John and Abigail's letters, it was best to harvest them during the warmer seasons as the soil was looser. As they grow on the roots of the plant, they needed to be pulled from the ground by hand. It was a tedious and dirty job. Abigail described the hard labor to her husband:

> If it is necessary to make any more draughts upon us the women must Reap the Harvests. I am willing to do my part. I believe I could gather Corn and Husk it, but I should make a poor figure at diging Potatoes.[19]

Mashed potatoes were commonly served in households. Surprisingly, mashed potatoes have not changed very much since John Adams's time. Both Hannah Glasse's *The Art of Cookery Made Plain and Easy* (1784 edition) and *Cookery Reformed: Or, the Lady's Assistant* (1755) recommend the same procedure. Modern-day recipes, like this one, speed up the process by noting that the potatoes should be diced before boiling.

5 medium sized potatoes, peeled and diced into 1-inch cubes
1 ½ cups milk
1 teaspoon salt
5 tablespoons unsalted butter

Put pototoes in a large pot and cover with water. Bring pot to a boil, and boil potatoes for about 20 to 25 minutes until they are tender.

Use a colander to drain the water from the pot, then put the potatoes back into the pot, and mash them well. Add the milk and salt, stirring well so potatoes do not stick to the pot. Add the butter, and stir.

During his early period in Europe, John Adams began to see a distinction between an elegant dinner in the city and a country-style dinner in the provinces. In his journal, John recorded details of a country dinner in Bordeaux.

> This Morning I took Leave of the Frigate Boston, and excepting a short Visit or two on board, before I satt out on my Journey to Paris never saw her afterwards. …I went up to the City of Bourdeaux with my Son and Servant, Mr. Vernon, Mr. Jesse Deane who were all my Suite, and Dr. Noel as an Interpreter, in the Pinnace. When We came up to the Town We had the good Luck to see Mr. McCreery and Major Fraser, on the Wharf. McCrery I had known in America. It had happened that I had ridden a long Journey with him. He came on board our Boat and conducted Us up to his Lodgings, where We dined, in the fashion of the Country. Among many other Things We had fish, and Salad, and Claret, Champaign and Mountain Wines. After Dinner Mr. Bondfield, whom I had known also in America, and who was agent at this place, invited me to a Walk. We went first to his Lodgings where We drank Tea, and then walked around the Town and went to see the new Comedy, a most splendid Building erecting for the Amusement of the Town.[20]

Few cookbooks described how salad was prepared at this time in history, but Joseph Gilliers's *Le Cannameliste Français*, published in 1768, was a French dictionary on basic culinary arts and listed several types of salad, or "*salade*," such as "potato salad," "small lettuce," "salad of celery," and "salad of citrus."

Salad has not changed much since the Pilgrims' time. Seventeenth-century cookbooks, such as Franciscus van Sterbeeck's *The Sensible Cook* or *De Verstandige Kock* (1668, Netherlands), included recipes on boiled salad greens Some salads would be served hot and others cold.[21]

As Abigail later noted in a letter to Mary Smith Cranch, salad was usually served as a side to meat dishes. The following salad recipe is based on a description from John Lawson's *A New Voyage to Carolina*, which published in 1709, and which stated, "The Sallads are the Lettice, Curl'd, Red, Cabbage, and Savoy. The Spinage round and prickly, Fennel…."[22]

Lettuce
Cabbage
Spinach
Savory
Parsley
Fennel

In a large mixing bowl, combine lettuce and other greens. Mix well with hands or two large spoons.

Serve with "salad sauce." (See recipe next page.)

For the sauce:
This recipe is based on William Kitchiner's *The Cook's Oracle* (1822 edition).

  3 hard-boiled eggs
  2 teaspoons water
  1 teaspoon ground mustard
  4 tablespoons white vinegar
  3 tablespoon olive oil or salad oil

Boil the eggs. Separate the whites and yolks. Set aside the egg whites for garnish.

Using a wooden spoon, crush the egg yolks through a sieve into a bowl.

Add water, ground mustard, white vinegar, and olive oil. Mix well. Toss with the salad just before eating.

When serving the salad, garnish with the egg whites.

Like a soldier who constantly wishes to be back at home from war, John Adams frequently wrote that he wished he were home on the family farm. In a letter to Abigail, he said:

> My Time might have been improved to some Purpose, in mowing Grass, raking Hay, or hoeing Corn, weeding Carrotts, picking or shelling Peas. [23]

Carrots were imported to the colonies by the East India Company in the mid-eighteenth century. By the latter part of the century, Thomas Jefferson was growing them on his farm at Monticello and suggesting they were a healthy supplement to the diet.

John Adams, too, grew carrots. In a 1764 letter to Cotton Tufts, he complained about the bugs eating his crops:

> My Gardens and my Farm, are complaining of Neglect, and Disorders, and all that: But I tell them, Patiens, Prudens—next Year I'le take better Care of Ye. Next Year, Ye shall have your Bellies full of Carrotts and Onions, and Beats, and Parsnips, and Cabbages and Potatoes, and every Thing that is good. But Ye must permit the little Villains call'd the small Pox to have their Feast this Spring. [24]

This recipe for boiled carrots was found in numerous cookbooks during Adams's time, including Francis Collingwood and John Woolams's *The Universal Cook and City and Country Housekeeper* (1792).

> If your carrots are young, you need only wipe them after they are boiled; but if they are old, you must scrape them before they are boiled. Slice them into a plate and pour melted butter over them. Young spring carrots will be boiled in half an hour, large ones in an hour, and old Sandwich carrots will take two hours. [25]

3-5 medium or large carrots
salt

Peel the carrots. Cut off any spoiled parts.

Slice the carrots. Boil them in a large pan with water until they turn bright orange. Add a pinch of salt for flavoring.

Serve in a large bowl.

Corn was a native crop in the colonies. When the English settlers arrived at Cape Cod, they searched the area for natives who might be able to help them. After surviving a harsh winter (with 102 deaths in their party), they found an area with fertile soil and discovered Indian corn. They named this area Corn Hill, and it was here that they established Plymouth Plantation.[26] Later, the Wampanoags taught the Separatists,[27] or Pilgrims, about the crop.

Corn became a staple in the colonists' diet and was consumed almost daily by John and Abigail. It could also be used as a cash crop. Frequently, Abigail corresponded with her husband and her cousin Cotton Tufts about the price of corn. Benjamin Franklin extolled the virtues of corn in an article titled "Homespun Celebrates Indian Corn," which appeared in *The Gazetteer and New Daily Advertiser.*

> Pray let me, an American, inform the gentleman, who seems quite ignorant of the matter, that Indian corn, take it for *all in all*, is one of the most agreeable and wholesome grains in the world; that its green ears roasted are a delicacy beyond expression; that *samp*, *hominy*, *succatash*, and *nokehock*, made of it, are so many pleasing varieties; and that a *johny*, or *hoe-cake*, hot from the fire, is better than a Yorkshire muffin.[28]

While corn was relatively easy to grow, maintaining it could be a tedious job. John Adams complained about the bugs destroying his corn:

> My Corn this Year, has been injured by two Species of Worms. One of the Size and Shape of a Catterpillar, but of a mouse Colour, lies at the root, eats off the Stalk and then proceeds to all the other Plants in the Hill, till he frequently kills them all. The other is long and slender as a needle, of a bright yellow Colour. He is found in the Center of the Stalk near the Ground where he eats it off, as the Hessian fly eats the Wheat. My Brother taught me, the Method of finding these Vermin, and destroying them. They lie commonly near the Surface.[29]

Like most vegetables, corn was boiled in the Adamses' time.

4 ears of corn
butter, salted or unsalted, to taste

Peel off the husks. Boil the corn in a large pot of water for about 5 minutes until it turns bright yellow. The center of the cob should turn clear.

Take a knife and slice a kernel off the cob to check for readiness.

Serve with butter.

Photo by Ed Nute

Photo by Ed Nute

CHAPTER 7

Soup

John and Abigail mentioned several types of soup in their writings. Soup was easy to make and easily fed a large group like the Adams family. While John Adams was in France, he observed the formality with which the French served soup as part of a meal. He later adopted this custom back at home, using tureens he purchased in France.

Covered tureens like this were used to serve soup at meals. This particular tureen was purchased by John and Abigail Adams while they were in France and was later used at their home, Peace field, as well as at state dinners in Washington during Adams's presidency. *Courtesy of National Park Service, Adams National Historical Park.*

The recipe for a typical English vegetable soup in John and Abigail Adames' time is based on John Farley's book *The London Art of Cookery* (1811 edition). The recipe does not include tomatoes, which were considered poisonous. Tomatoes were not used for culinary purposes in the what would become the United States until the early nineteenth century, when they were introduced by Thomas Jefferson. While touring Italy during his tenure as minister to France in the late 1780s, Jefferson sampled many foods that were new to him. He learned that the tomato originated in South America but had been introduced to southern Europe almost two hundred years before Jefferson arrived. He took seeds back home to grow in his experimental garden at Monticello.

Tomatoes owed their bad reputation to the fact that they were often served on pewter ware. The high concentration of lead in the pewter ware and the high concentration of acidity in tomatoes created a chemical reaction that could cause lead poisoning over time. Today, if pewter ware is produced, it has a wax coating on it so it is safe for food consumption.

This vegetable soup is cooked with beef bones and small bits of beef. One may substitute pork or chicken. Modern alterations to the recipe includethe addition of two tablespoons of butter.

3 ½ pints water
1 large white onion
1 bunch celery
½ purple top turnip
1 pound carrots
1 pound beef ribs or beef bone marrow
2 tablespoons unsalted butter (or olive oil)
1 tablespoon table salt
½ tablespoon ground black pepper

Dice all the vegetables. Divide the diced vegetables in half.

Wash the beef ribs.

Fill a large pot with 9 cups of water, and place half the vegetables, the meat, the butter, and salt and pepper in the pot.

Let the soup stew gently at medium heat, for 1 ½ to 2 hours.

When the meat is tender, its color will change. Strain off the bones and vegetables.

Add the other half of the diced vegetables to the strained broth. Simmer briefly until vegetables are tender.

As Farley notes: "Adding fresh vegetables cut in the form of a dice; simmer till tender, and serve." [1]

While sailing to Europe, Abigail Adams wrote to her sister Mary on Sunday, July 25, 1784: "We had a handsome dinner of salt fish pea soup Boild fowl and tongue roast and fry'd Lamb, with a pudding and fruit."[2]

This recipe for pea soup is based on *The Lady's Companion: Or, An Infallible Guide* (1743 edition).

3 cups water
12 ounces frozen peas or 2 ¼ cups dried split peas
1 stalk mint
½ tablespoon marjoram leaves
½ tablespoon thyme
2 tablespoons butter
¼ cup spinach

Combine all ingredients a 4-quart pan. Boil at low heat for two hours. Stir occasionally.

Based on Elizabeth Cleland's *A New and Easy Method of Cookery* (1755), this recipe uses homemade beef broth. You can substitute prepared low-sodium beef broth.

1 pound beef shin
5 cups water
1 small onion, chopped
1½ teaspoons salt
1 pinch ground allspice
¾ teaspoon ground mace
¼ teaspoon ground cloves
½ teaspoon dried marjoram
½ teaspon dried basil
2 cucumbers (pared and cut into slices 1/2-inch thick)
2 tablespoons unsalted butter

Boil beef shin for about 45 minutes.
Skim out extra fats by pouring the liquid into another sauce pan through a sieve. Return pan to heat.

Add the chopped onion.

Then add salt, allspice, mace, cloves, marjoram, and basil. Cook about 15 minutes at medium heat.

In a separate pan, stew cucumber slices in butter briefly.

Add cucumbers and butter into the beef broth, and cook at low heat for about two hours. Stir slowly and regularly.

Housewives like Abigail learned how to determine the freshness of fish. In Amelia Simmons' *American Cookery* (1796), she advised the following:

> Experience and attention will dictate the choice of the best. Fresh gills, full bright eyes, moist fins and tails denotements of their being fresh caught; if they are soft, its certain they are stale, but if deceits are used, your smell must approve or denounce them, and be your safest guide.

This cod stew recipe is based on Lucy Emerson's *The New England Cookery*, which was published in 1808 and was a plagiarized version of Amelia Simmons's work.

5 raw oysters, cleaned and prepared
1 pound cod fillet, skinned and deboned
½ sweet onion, chopped.
¼ cup water
¾ cup white wine
1 large stalk fresh marjoram, leaves only, crushed
½ teaspoon summer savory
½ teaspoon ground nutmeg
½ teaspoon dried thyme or 2 stalks fresh thyme, leaves only
½ teaspoon ground pepper
salt, to taste, about 3 pinches
3 tablespoons unsalted butter
2 teaspoons flour
½ teaspoon ground mace
1 tablespoon lemon juice

Photo by Ed Nute

Clean the oysters and open them. Remove them from the shells, and put them into a bowl.

Cut the cod into 1-inch thick pieces. In a pot, combine fish, oysters, onion, water, and white wine. Bring to a boil, then add the herbs (listed from marjoram through thyme), ground pepper, and about 3 pinches of salt. Boil for 5-10 minutes at medium heat.

As the stew continue to cook at medium heat, stir slowly.

Add in the unsalted butter and sprinkle in flour to thicken the mixture.

Add a pinch of mace and lemon juice. Add additional salt, to taste.

Before serving, remove any stalks from the herbs.

John wrote to his son John Quincy Adams, who was abroad on diplomatic affairs, on August 27, 1815, that he encouraged the boys (George Washington Adams and John Adams II) to "disarrange all the Papers on my writing Table…devour all my Strawberries, Cherries, Currants, Plumb, Peaches, Pears and Apples." *Photo by Ed Nute*

CHAPTER 8

Puddings and Snacks

Pudding was a staple food for the working class and lower class throughout New England and for the sick. In a letter to his future wife, Abigail Smith, in April of 1764, John Adams described his meal the night before his smallpox inoculation.

> The Dr. came, immediately with Dr. Warren, in a Chaise—And after an Apology, for his not Recollecting-(I am obliged to break off my Narration, in order to swallow a Porringer of Hasty Pudding and Milk. I have done my Dinner) —for not recollecting what Dr. Tufts had told him, Dr. Perkins demanded my left Arm and Dr. Warren my Brothers.[1]

In his letters to his future wife, Abigail, John Adams often described what type of pudding he had. The pudding was usually served along with a main dish.

On October 26, 1799, Abigail described to her husband a traditional New England dinner of thanksgiving:

> The day was not forgotten by me. Mrs. Smith invited Mr. Otis and Family to dine with us upon the occasion, and made the token of New England thanksgiving a fine plumb pudding, and the company toasted the day and many happy returns of it.[2]

Plumb, or plum, pudding was one of the couple's favorite dishes.

On a passage to France, Abigail wrote, " In short I have been obliged to turn cook myself and have made two puddings, the only thing I have seen fit to eat."[3]

Plum pudding dated back to fifteenth-century England. It was traditionally served during the first course of a meal. Some sources say the Puritans rejected plum pudding as it had too many exotic spices and was not purified in accordance with their religious beliefs. However, by the early 1800s, the younger generations became more liberal about exploring different exotic spices brought by the East India Company. Plum pudding became a favorite during the holidays, particularly for the Adams family.

This recipe is based on several historical cookbooks, including Mary Eaton's *The Cook and Housekeeper's Complete and Universal Dictionary* (1823), which included boiled and baked versions.

Serves 3-4

1 orange
1 lemon
About 3 slices of wheat bread, finely shredded
4 tablespoons butter, softened, plus more for pan
¾ cup raisins
1 cup currants
6 eggs
1 cup flour
2 tablespoons ground nutmeg
2 teaspoon ground mace
2 teaspoons ground cinnamon
1 teaspoon salt
½ cup whole milk
⅔ cup sugar
¼ cup brandy

Preheat the oven to 300 degrees.

Shred the lemon and orange peels into a bowl. Set aside.

In a large bowl, mix the bread pieces, raisins, currants, eggs, and flour. Add the nutmeg, mace, cinnamon, salt, milk, sugar, brandy, and the shredded peels.

Grease a cake pan with butter. Pour the mixture into the pan. Cover it with aluminum foil. Bake for about an hour.

Cut the pudding into slices. Serve with plum pudding sauce, if desired.

For the pudding sauce:
The following is based on William Kitchiner's *The Cook's Oracle: And Housekeeper's Manual* (1822 edition).

1 ½ tablespoons butter, melted
½ cup brandy
½ cup sherry
⅓ cup sugar

In a sauce pan, melt the butter. Add the brandy and sherry.

Then add the sugar and sweeten to your preference. Boil for a few minutes.

Serve in a small bowl.

Here's another example of a pudding John and Abigail might have enjoyed. It includes an optional recipe for melted butter with sugar, used as a sauce for the pudding. It is based on Richard Briggs' *The English Art of Cookery* (1788) and Charles Carter's *The London and Country Cook* (1749).

Serves 4-5

2 ½ pints heavy cream
3 tablespoons orange flower water
About 2 or 3 pinches ground mace
½ cup sugar
2 tablespoons sherry
1 cup sliced or slivered blanched almonds
½ teaspoon salt
2 eggs, beaten
3 tablespoons flour
2 tablespoons butter, plus more for pan

Preheat oven to 350 degrees.

Stir all the ingredients in a large mixing bowl.

Grease a cake pan with butter. Pour the mixture into the cake pan. Bake for about 30 minutes.

The pudding is done when a knife poked into the center comes out clean.

Put a plate over the cake pan, then flip it upside down so the cake is on the plate.

For the butter sauce:

16 tablespoons unsalted butter
½ cup sugar

In a pot, melt the butter over medium heat. Be careful not to brown or burn the butter.

Whisk in the sugar. Continue to whisk until the sugar disappears. Pour into a bowl.

This was a popular dish among New England households. John Adams mentioned it once in a letter to Louisa Catherine Adams, John Quincy Adams's wife, about New Year's Eve fare at the family table. "...Eating fat Turkeys, roast Beef and Indian Pudding..."[4] The following recipe is from Hannah Glasse's *The Art of Cookery Made Plain and Easy*, which was reprinted in 1805 for American readers.

Butter for pan
3 cups milk
1 cup corn meal
½ cup molasses
1 teaspoon salt

Preheat the oven to 350 degrees. Butter a cake pan.

Scald the milk in a 4-quart pan at 180 degrees. Stir constantly to prevent any burning or solidifying. Check the temperature with a meat thermometer.

Remove the pan from the heat. Stir in the corn meal. Add the molasses and the salt.

Pour the mixture into the cake pan. Bake for about 45 minutes. Serve on a large plate.

A note on fruit and nut snacks

John and Abigail enjoyed snacks such as fruits, nuts, and candied goods.

They enjoyed working in their home garden, where they grew a variety of fruits. John also frequently mentioned in his diaries different types of fruits that he saw on this travels.

> Went this Morning to Mr. Boylstones, to make a wedding Visit to Mr. Gill and his Lady. A very cordial, polite, and friendly Reception, I had. Mr. Gill shewed me Mr. Boylstones Garden, and a large, beautifull and agreable one it is—a great Variety of excellent fruit, Plumbs, Pears, Peaches, Grapes, Currants &c. &c—a figg Tree, &c.[5]

In his diary, he also once wrote about watermelons.

> [Colburn] Barrell this Morning at Breakfast entertained Us with an Account of his extravagant Fondness for Fruit. When he lived at New market he could get no fruit but Strawberries, and he used frequently to eat 6 Quarts in a Day. At Boston, in the very hottest of the Weather he breakfasts upon Water Melons—neither Eats nor drinks any Thing else for Breakfast. In the Season of Peaches he buys a Peck, every Morning, and eats more than half of them himself. In short he eats so much fruit in the Season of it that he has very little Inclination to any other Food.[6]

Abigail found working in the garden to be therapeutic. She was proud of her work. In a May 8, 1801, letter to Catherine Nuth Johnson (mother of Louisa Catherine Johnson and mother-in-law of John Quincy Adams), she wrote:

> The Beaties which my garden unfolds to my view from the window at which I now write tempt me to forget the past, and rejoice in the full bloom of the pear, the Apple, the plumb and peach, and the rich luxuriance of the grass plots, interspersed with the cowslip and daffy, and Callombine, all unite to awake the most pleasing sensations.[7]

Photo by Ed Nute

Apples played a major role in the Adams family's working garden. Abigail oversaw all the farm work and projects. While away in Jamaica, New York, in December 1788, she instructed her husband: "The cider Should be drawn off, and my Pears and Apples picked over and repack'd."[8]

Prunes was also a favorite in the Adams household. They frequently mentioned having "plumb pudding" and "Plumb cake." Raisins and other candried fruits were also popular during their time.

John and Abigail rarely specified the types of nuts they consumed, but almonds would most likely have been a favorite in the Adams household. They could be found in various dishes, such as almond pudding (see page 97). When John Adams was in Philadelphia during the Second Continental Congress, he wrote about having almonds as dessert at Benjamin Chew's home:

> Dined with Mr. Chew, Chief Justice of the Province, with all the Gentlemen from Virginia, Dr. Shippen, Mr. Tilghman and many others. We were shewn into a grand Entry and Stair Case, and into an elegant and most magnificent Chamber, untill Dinner. About four O Clock We were called down to Dinner. The Furniture was all rich.—Turttle, and every other Thing—Flummery, Jellies, Sweetmeats of 20 sorts, Trifles, Whip'd Syllabubbs, floating Islands, fools—&c., and then a Desert of Fruits, Raisins, Almonds, Pears, Peaches....[9]

Walnuts and chestnuts were also popular in the Colonial period. In one of John's diary entries in November of 1766, he wrote about trimming walnuts in his "common pasture."[10]

Candied fruits were another popular snack or dessert, and another favorite among the Adamses. They were made while the fruits were in season, and then could be saved for the colder months. Some fruits were frequently candied because they were so rare to the region, including oranges and lemons. Abigail relied on acquaintances and family members, including Cotton Tufts, to help her acquire specific produce. She could have used lemon and orange peels to make candied fruits after she squeezed the juice out to make punch.

Photo by Ed Nute

CHAPTER 9

As a grandmother, Abigail often wrote about how her grandchildren craved pies more than the main dishes at meals. John Adams enjoyed dessert, too. In his diary in September of 1774, he wrote:

> Attended my Duty on the Committee all Day, and a most ingenious, entertaining Debate We had.—The happy News was bro't us, from Boston, *that* no Blood *had been spill'd* but that Gen. Gage had taken away the Provincial Powder from the Magazine at Cambridge. This last was a disagreable Circumstance. Dined at Mr. Powells, with Mr. Duché, Dr. Morgan, Dr. Steptoe, Mr. Goldsborough, Mr. Johnson, and many others.—A most sinfull Feast again! Every Thing which could delight the Eye, or allure the Taste, Curds and Creams, Jellies, Sweet meats of various sorts, 20 sorts of Tarts, fools, Trifles, floating Islands, whippd Sillabubs &c. &c.—Parmesan Cheese, Punch, Wine, Porter, Beer &c. &c.
>
> At Evening We climbed up the Steeple of Christ Church, with Mr. Reed, from whence We had a clear and full View of the whole City and of Delaware River.[1]

In one of her letters to her sister Mary, written early in Abigail's marriage to John, Abigail wrote, "My Good Man is so very fat that I am lean as a rail."[2] Later, in his first term as vice president, John would be nicknamed "His Rotundity."

Baked Custard

Baked custard has been a popular dessert since the Adamses' time. They baked it in stoneware. As William Kitchiner wrote in *The Cook's Oracle* (1822 edition), "Fill it in earthen cups, and bake them immediately in a hot oven to give them a good colour…"

The following is a modernized version of his recipe. Instead of using stoneware, try three 10-ounce ceramic ramekins.

- 2 cups whole milk
- 3 eggs, beat
- ½ cups sugar
- 1 teaspoon cinnamon, ground
- 1 teaspoon coriander seed
- A few tablespoons lemon peel, zest

Preheat oven to 300 degrees. Set up the ramekins in a large pan filled with water.

Boil the milk in a saucepan until it scalds.

In a large mixing bowl, combine the other ingredients. Pour the mixture into the scalded milk. Stir it until all the ingredients are well mixed.

Pour mixture into the ramekins. Put ramekins, still in the water-filled pan, in the oven and bake for about 30 minutes, until the custard becomes solid. Test by sticking a knife into the center; when the custard is done the knife will come out clean.

According to the *Oxford English Dictionary*, fruit fool dates back to 1598. For John Adams's generation, desserts like this were served primarily at the tables of the wealthy class. This recipe is a modern version based on recipes from Eliza Smith's *The Compleat Housewife* (1739 edition) and Mary Eaton's 1823 cookbook dictionary.

  1 cup fresh strawberries, washed and hulled
  1 tablespoon orange flower water
  1 cup heavy whipping cream (pasteurized)
  2 tablespoons powdered sugar

Mash the strawberries with a citrus reamer or potato smasher. Stir in the orange flower water.

In another bowl, whisk the cream with the sugar until it develop soft peaks.

Fold in the strawberry mixture.

Massachusetts housewives like Abigail Adams learned to use cranberries for the main course, desserts, and sauces. As the editor of *American Farmer Containing Original Essays and Selections on Rural Economy* (1823), John S. Skinner included an essay on cranberries.

> This is one of the best fruits in the world. All tarts sink out of sight, in point of merit, when compared with that made of the American Cranberry. There is a little dark red thing, about as big as a large pea, sent to England from north of Europe, and is called a Cranberry; but it does not resemble the American in taste any more than in bulk—It is well known that this valuable fruit is, in many parts of this country, spread over the low lands in great profusion; and that the mere gathering of it is all that bountiful nature requires at our hands.—This fruit is preserved all the year, by stewing and putting into jars, and when taken thence is better than currant jelly.

Cranberry tart recipes did not come into cookbooks until the later part of the 1700s and the early 1800s.

The crust for this type of fruit tart is a sugar crust shell. Julia Child has a good recipe for this type of shell in *Mastering the Art of French Cooking*. Or, you can buy sugar crust shell in the frozen food section of the grocery store. Since this recipe calls for fresh cranberries, it might be best if you make your own crust.

Hannah Glasse's *The Art of Cookery Made Plain and Easy* (1784 reprint) gave a recipe for tart paste: "One Pound of flour, three quarters of a pound of butter; mix up together, and beat well with a rolling-pin."

The following recipe is based on the works of M. Radcliffe's *A Modern System of Domestic Cookery* (1823) and Amelia Simmons' *American Cookery* (1796).

1 bag (1 pound) fresh or frozen cranberries
½ cup sugar
Premade tart crust

Preheat oven to 325 degrees.

If using frozen cranberries, defrost, then place in a large bowl. With a large spoon, smash them to help remove any excess liquid.

Rinse the cranberries.

Sprinkle sugar evenly on the tart crust. Spread the cranberries evenly on the tart crust.

Bake for about 15 to 20 minutes until the crust turns golden brown. Cool before refrigerating or serving.

For the Tart Crust:
The following is based on Richard Briggs' *English Art of Cookery (*1788):

  1 cup flour
  ½ cup sugar
  5 tablespoons unsalted butter
  1 tablespoon ice water
  1 egg yolk (beaten)

In a large mixing bowl, with your hands or with a fork, mix the flour, sugar, and butter until it achieves an oatmeal-like texture. If using an electric mixer, mix for just a few seconds.

Add the water and the egg yolk into the mixture. Mix.

Wrap the dough in a plastic wrap or parchment paper. Refrigerate for several hours or overnight.

After taking the dough out of the refrigerator, on a cold surface, briskly beat it with a rolling pin. Roll it out thin to about an inch. Sprinkle on additional flour if necessary to prevent sticking.

Transfer the dough to an 8-inch tart pan (try using the rolling pin to roll up the dough and then unroll it into the pan).

Remove excess dough.

Use a fork to poke holes in the dough. This is to allow the crust to breathe as it bakes in the oven.

After one of her first dinners in England, in July of 1784, Abigail reported to her sister Mary Smith Cranch:

> I returnd and dined with Mrs. Atkinson by her invitation the Evening before, in company with Mr. Smith, Mrs. Hay, Mr. Appleton. We had a turbot; a Soup and a roast leg of Lamb, with a cherry pye.[3]

Many people think that cherry pie is an American invention, but it was eaten in England dating back to Elizabethan times. Numerous English cookbook authors, including Hannah Glasse and Richard Briggs, had cherry pie among their recipes. English settlers introduced cherry pie to the New World, and ultimately it became one of America's favorite recipes.

To recreate the kind of cherry pie that Abigail had in London, try this modern interpretation of two recipes, one from from Hannah Glasse's *The Art of Cookery Made Plain and Easy* (1784 edition) and one from *Cookery Reformed: Or, the Lady's Assistant,* (1755).

For this recipe, you'll need to pit the cherries. Get a bottle with a small mouth, such as a beer bottle, and a chopstick. Remove the stems and rinse the cherries. Place the cherry with the head facing up in the mouth of the bottle. Use the thick end of the chopstick to press down on the cherry. The seed will pop into the bottle.

Making pie crusts from scratch has not changed much since Abigail's time. There are several ways to make the crust for dessert pies. "Puff-Paste" was one of the popular kinds of crust wrote Hannah Glasse in The *Art of Cookery Made Plain and Easy* (1784 edition). This crust recipe is based on the one in her book.

For the crust:

16 tablespoons unsalted butter or 1 cup vegetable shortening
1 tablespoon salt
2 ½ cups all-purpose flour, plus more for work surface
6 tablespoons ice water

Dice the butter or shortening into cubes. In a large bowl, mix the butter, salt, and flour. Sprinkle ice water, one tablespoon at a time, into the mixture, incorporating the water into the mixture. Knead the mixture briefly if you need to, just to get all the flour well mixed. Pack the dough into a large ball.

Divide the dough in two halves. Place each half separately in an airtight bag and refrigerate for one day.

Flour the work area.

Take one of the dough portions out of its bag. Knead the dough briefly. Roll the dough thin, to about one-eighth inch in thickness. Press down gently as you use a rolling pin to roll the dough. Flour the dough if it gets sticky.

Transfer the dough to an 8-inch pie pan. Trim any extra dough. (You can use any extra dough for the next step.)

Crimp the edges of the crust or use a fork to make some sort of pattern. Put the pie crust in the refrigerator to keep it cool while repeating the same procedure to prepare the other dough portion for the top crust.

For the pie:

    3 ½ cups fresh, pitted cherries
    4 tablespoons granulated sugar, divided
    1 egg white
    2 teaspoons water

Place a baking sheet in the middle rack of the oven. Preheat oven to 450 degrees.

Take the bottom pie crust out of the refrigerator and let it sit at room temperature for about 10 minutes. Poke holes in the crust dough randomly with a fork.

In a bowl, mix the cherries with 2 tablespoons sugar.

Sprinkle the other 2 tablespoons of sugar inside the crust. Pour the pitted, sugared cherries into the crust.

Place the second crust on top of the berries. Seal the edges using a small amount of water. Optional: Extra dough can be used to decorate the top. Patterns can range from hearts to leaves. Apply dough decorations using a small amount of water to keep them in place.

Mix egg white and water in a small bowl to create a wash.

Use a pastry brush to glaze the top crust with the egg white wash.

Place the pie on the baking sheet in the middle rack of the oven; bake 10 minutes. Then reduce the heat to 350 degrees and bake for 30 minutes or until the crust turns golden brown.

Take the pie out of the oven. Let it cool for 20 minutes. Serve cold.

Throughout most of his life, John Adams kept a journal. When he worked in Europe, he gave up this habit, but he picked it back up briefly in the 1800s. In one of his entries in 1756, he wrote, "Election Day. I have spent all this Day at Home reading a little and eating a little Election Cake."[4]

The following recipe is based on Amelia Simmons's *American Cookery* (1796) and Maria Lydia Child's *The American Frugal Housewife* (1833 edition).

8 tablespoons (1 stick) unsalted butter, softened, plus more for cake pan
2 ½ cups flour
1 cup raisins
1 teaspoon ground allspice
4 teaspoons ground coriander seeds
3 teaspoons ground cinnamon
⅔ cup sugar
1 package fast-acting yeast
3 tablespoons brandy
2 tablespoons white wine
2 eggs, beaten
⅔ cup white milk (2%)

Grease a fluted cake pan with butter.

Cut the butter into small cubes. In a large mixing bowl, sift the flour, then mix in the butter and all the dry ingredients (raisins through sugar).

Prepare the yeast according to directions on the package.

Add the yeast, brandy, wine, eggs and milk to the dry ingredients. Mix well.

Pour the mixture into the prepared cake pan. Cover with plastic wrap. Set in a cool area to allow the batter to rise for about 8 to 10 hours.

Preheat the oven to 375 degrees.

Bake for about 30 to 40 minutes.

Cake is done when a toothpick or knife inserted in its center comes out clean.

While in Paris in April of 1778, John Adams wrote in his diary, and in a letter to Pieter van Bleiswyck, about the cake he shared with Benjamin Franklin and others.

> "We Were invited to dine at Monsieur Brillons, a Family in which Mr. Franklin was very intimate, and in which he spent much of his Time. Here We met a large Company of both Sexes and among them were Monsieur Le Vailliant and his Lady. Madam Brillion was one of the most beautiful Women in France, a great Mistress of Musick, as were her two little Daughters. The Dinner was Luxury, as usual in that Country. A large Cake was brought in with three flags flying."[5]

John wrote that one of the flags was inscribed "Haec Dies" (pride subdued), while the others read "in qua fit Congressus" and "exultemus et potemus in e," which all together translated as a call to rejoice and drink to celebrate the actions of Congress.

This recipe for "Gâteau à la Dauphine" comes from Mrs. Dalgairns's *The Practice of Cookery: Adapted to the Business of Every Day Life* (1830). It was based on a recipe found in Menon and Rougnard's *La Science du maître-d'hôtel cuisinier, avec des observations sur la connoissance et les propriétés des alimens* (1789), or *The Science of Steward Cook, with observations on the knowledge and properties of the food*.

The Age of Enlightenment, which centered on the seventeenth and eighteenth centuries, was a time of change philosophically and politically, and these changes were reflected in the culinary world. Desserts such as cakes were no longer relegated to the upper classes but became a favorite of all social levels. Cooks and chefs took the opportunity to extend their creativity in making these desserts. First Lady Martha Washington was highly praised for her cake and tea time, setting an example for her successor, Abigail Adams.

For the cake:
1 package of yeast
2 ¼ cups all-purpose flour
8 egg yolks
2 egg whites
¼ cup water
2 tablespoons rose water
½ cup sugar
12 tablespoons butter, plus more for greasing the pan

Preheat oven to 325 degrees.

Prepare the yeast in a separate bowl, according to package directions.

In a large bowl, combine the flour, egg yolks, egg whites, water, rose water, sugar and butter. Mix well. (Save the rest of the eggs whites for the icing.)

Grease the cake pan with butter. Pour the batter into the pan. Place the cake pan into the oven, and bake for 30-40 minutes.

Cool cake on a cake rack before icing.

For the icing:
This recipe is based upon Hannah Glasse's *The Art of Cookery Made Plain and Easy* (1784 edition).

   Powdered sugar
   6 egg whites
   Flower water

In a large mixing bowl, combine the ingredients, then whisk until the mixture thickens. Spread on the cake.

In his diary, John Adams mentioned having whipped cream (or "whipt" cream, as it was often spelled in those days) while at dinner in Philadelphia during his time as a delegrate to Congress. Whipped cream was often used at that time as a dip for fruits or sweetmeats and was served over tarts.

Without modern appliances, whipping the cream was hard work. Sometimes wine would be added to the whipped cream. In this recipe, adding wine is optional. Only a minimal amount is added to provide flavor.

Recipes from cookbooks of the Adamses' days might call for musk or ambergris to perfume the cream. Ambergris was a popular culinary ingredient in the eighteenth century. It is a waxy substance made from the intestines of the sperm whale.[6] Musk is a strong-smelling substance from an Asiatic deer.

Cookbook author John Farley suggested including "sack" when preparing whipped cream. This is a type of Spanish dry wine fortified with brandy, such as sherry, amontillado, or canary.

Makes 1 cup

    1 large bowl of ice and water
    2 egg whites
    1 cup (½ pint) heavy whipping cream
    2 pieces lemon peel
    Optional: 2 tablespoons sherry
    5-6 tablespoons powdered sugar, to taste

Set up a bowl of ice and water to go underneath your mixing bowl, which should be about 9 or 10 inches in diameter and about 5 or 6 inches deep. This will keep the ingredients cool during the manual whipping process.

Beat the egg whites and the heavy whipping cream in the large mixing bowl with a large balloon whisk, 5 to 6 inches in diameter. Add two slices of lemon peel for flavor.

Optional: Whip in the sherry.

Add the powdered sugar as you continue to beat the egg whites with the balloon whip. You may add more if you like the whipped cream sweeter. When the cream is thick, remove the lemon peel.

Keep refrigerated.

Syllabub was a popular dessert in the eighteenth century. Traditional English syllabub is milk or cream curdled with alcohol.

It was so popular that images of syllabub can be found in political cartoons, such as James Gilray's "Heroes recruiting at Kelseys" (1798). Generally, syllabub would be served in a glass about 4.5 inches tall and with a small spoon to scoop out the cream. The Adamses had syllabub frequently, especially at formal dinner engagements, and both wrote about the dessert.

John and Abigail might have enjoyed "syllabub under the cow," in which the fresh cow's milk was squeezed right into the alcohol. To get the same frothy effect today, one could squeeze milk out of something like a ketchup bottle into the mixing bowl, according to Gavin R. Nathan, author of *Historic Taverns of Boston*.

In a letter to her niece Lucy Cranch Greenleaf[7] written on August 27, 1785, Abigail described a typical, grand-style dinner:

> It is usual at a large entertainment, to bring the solid food in the first course. The second consists of lighter diet, kickshaws, trifles, whip syllabub, &c.; the third is the dessert, consisting of the fruits of the season, and sometimes foreign sweetmeats.[8]

Photo by Ed Nute

This recipe combines ideas from several books, including John Farley's *The London Art of Cookery* (1811 edition) and M. Radcliffe's *A Modern System of Domestic Cookery* (1823).

½ medium-size lemon, juice and finely grated rind
1 pint heavy whipping cream (pasteurized)
¼ cup brandy
2 tablespoon orange flower water
2 egg whites
⅔ cup powdered sugar
Sweet table wine, red or white or both, such as Reisling or Rhine.

Squeeze the lemon juice into a bowl and set aside.

In a large mixing bowl, whisk the whipping cream, brandy, orange-flower water, egg whites, grated lemon rind, and 3 tablespoons of lemon juice.

Add the powdered sugar into the mixture to taste. Whisk the mixture until it develops soft peaks.

Pour wine into glasses, then scoop cream on top. "Half-fill your glasses with some red, and some white wine, and with a spoon put on your syllabub as high as you can…"[9]

Refrigerate for about an hour, then serve immediately.

Photo by Ed Nute

CHAPTER 10

Alcoholic drinks played a major role in Colonial America. Water was considered unsafe to drink, so children were given fermented drinks. (When tea was boiled with water, they thought that the tea made the water safer to drink; what they didn't understand that it was the boiling of the water that made it safer to drink.)

In his student days at Harvard, John Adams enjoyed cider. Later, as president of the United States, he started his mornings with "a Jill of Cyder" (about four ounces) and wrote frequently of drinks he enjoyed at dinners.

In his diary, he wrote:

> In conformity to the fashion I drank this Morning and Yesterday Morning, about a Jill of Cyder. It seems to do me good, by diluting and dissolving the Phlegm or the Bile in the Stomach.[1]

Like many women of her time, Abigail grew up learning how to gather apples and press them into hard cider. During the Revolutionary War, John wrote to Abigail:

> Cyder will be our only Resource. However We must drink Water, and Milk, and We should live better, be healthier, and fight bolder than We do with our poisonous Luxuries.[2]

When he and Abigail moved to their new home at Peace field, John even had a "cider house" built on the property.

But John was opposed to drinking in excess. His brother-in-law William Smith died of alcoholism., as did John's son Charles. John's youngest son, Thomas Boylston Adams, also was a victim of alcoholism, though it did not kill him.

Even on one of his summer vacations from his work as vice-president, Adams complained about one of his drunken workers, Billings:

> Running to all the Shops and private Houses swilling Brandy, Wine and Cyder in quantities enough to destroy him. If the Ancients drank Wine as our People drink rum and Cyder it is no wonder We read of so many possessed with Devils.[3]

In a letter to Abigail, John wrote:

> I drank no Cyder, but feast upon Phyladelphia Beer, and Porter. A Gentleman, one Mr. [Robert] Hare, has lately set up in this City a Manufactory of Porter, as good as any that comes from London. I pray We may introduce it into the Massachusetts. It agrees with me, infinitely better than Punch, Wine, or Cyder, or any other Spirituous Liquor.[4]

In his diary, on September 14, 1774, John Adams wrote about a dinner with a few members of the Committee of Congress. Dr. Cox, Dr. Morgan, Dr. Rush, Mr. Bayard, and "old Mr. Smith."

> The Gentlemen entertained us, with Absurdities in the Laws of Pensylvania, New Jersey and Maryland. This I find is a genteel Topic of Conversation here. – A mighty Feast again, nothing less than the very best of Claret, Madeira, and Burgundy.

Throughout his diaries, John recorded different types of wines he consumed.

Madeira is a Portuguese wine and was often used in cooking. Port and sherry were also popular drinks. When traveling in Spain, John recorded different libations he found at the market.

While in France, John enjoyed many different types of wine, such as claret and bordeaux. In his autobiography, John described one of the grand meals he enjoyed shortly after he arrived in France, on March 31, 1778: "a little glass of French Liqueur. Wine and Water and excellent Claret with our dinner."[5]

During the last year of his presidency, John Adams wrote to Abigail about how madeira helped him to treat a minor cold:

> I came home and went into a warm bed and had a fine Perspiration, occasioned I believe by my drinking three Glasses of Madeira Wine at supper and two more after I came home, which has relieved me from all cold and I feel very well this morning.[152]

Brandy also played an important role in the Adamses' household. Abigail flavored brandy with lemon. In a letter to Sarah Livingston Jay, on February 20, 1789, she wrote:

> I reachd Home Ten days after I left Newyork. we had an agreeable journey, good Roads fine weather and tolerable accomodations, our Musk and Lemon Brandy were of great service to us, and we never faild to Toast the donor, Whilst our Hearts were warmed by the Recollection.[7]

Toasting to one's health was common etiquette during John Adams's time. In his retirement, John continued to celebrate the anniversary of the signing of Treaty of Paris in September 3, 1783. In a letter to his close friend Dr. Benjamin Rush, John wrote, "And as long as we Antediluvians can drink, we will toast Dr. Rush his Family and Friends, the 3d. of Sept. 1783 and the third of Septr. 1812."[8]

A note on tea

English colonists brought their love of tea drinking to America. Tea was among the major imports to the New World from southern regions of China, and throughout his diaries, John frequently described having tea with his guests.

Tea became more expensive due to British taxation known as the Tea Act. Although the Adamses adopted coffee as alternative drink, they sometimes still purchased tea. In a letter to John Adams, Abigail reported the price of tea.

> I hope you will not think me extravagant, I could account for the expenditure of every shilling to your satisfaction; I will give you one instance of prices here. Yesterday I gave 12 pounds Lawfull Money for one pound of Bohea tea.[9]

When rebels dumped tea into the Boston Harbor in protest to the Tea Act, John praised them for their patriotism.

> This Destruction of the Tea is so bold, so daring, so firm, intrepid and inflexible, and it must have so important Consequences, and so lasting, that I cant but consider it as an Epocha in History.[10]

After the revolution, tea became widely popular. As the wife of the vice president, Abigail Adams was frequently invited to the president's mansion to have tea with First Lady Martha Washington. Later, as the First Lady herself, Abigail would often host teas.

Abigail's daugther-in-law, Louisa Catherine Adams, once wrote about how she commented to Abigail and Abigail's sister Mary Smith Cranch about how much sugar the sisters took in their tea, which caused a row: "I had ventured to say that I thought they used more Sugar than was right—They insisted that they only took three piled spoonfuls in every Cup of tea, and as they were not accustomed to have things measured out to them...."[11]

John lived for eight years after Abigail's death. Louisa Catherine Adams helped take care of her aging father-in-law. On August 14, 1821, she hosted a reception for 200 West Point cadets who came to pay a visit to the former president and patriot.

Louisa, who was born in London, used this opportunity to promote her European-style entertaining and used her "cooking education, in consequence of having been a favorite of a very superior Cuisiniere in my fathers family."[12]

She recorded some of the details from this event: "We were all set up at six and the Tables were spread with refreshments. Three tables were spread in the Paddock between the Stables and the House with Hams, Tongues, Beef, Cheese, bread, crackers, Coffee, Chocolate, Limonade, Punch and wine."[15]

Lemonade has been a favorite American drink since the Colonial period. It was considered a social drink for dinner parties and other engagements. It was often served with cake.

The following is based on Elizabeth Raffald's *The Experienced English Housekeeper* (1818 edition) and Francis Collingwood and John Woolams' *The Universal Cook* (1792).

Fresh squeezed juice from 6 lemons
Fresh squeezed juice from 1 Seville orange
2 cups warm water
3 tablespoons orange flower water
1 cup sugar
Slices of lemon rind
Slices of Seville orange rind

Squeeze the lemon juice and orange juice into a bowl. Stir in the water, flower water, and sugar. Add additional sugar to taste.

Add lemon and orange rinds. Cover the bowl, and place mixture in the refrigerator for about an hour or two.

Use a jelly bag to strain juice, separating seeds until the juice looks clear. Serve cold.

In a letter to Abigail on May 14, 1777, John said that inflation in Philadelphia was so high, that when he offered drinks to his colleagues, he was "reduced to the Necessity of treating them with plain Toddy and Rum and Water—a Glass of Wine, once in a while to a great stranger, of uncommon Consideration."[14]

There are two popular versions of toddy that were served throughout the British colonies. The cold version was introduced from India and was known as "tart" in Hindi. The hot version originated in Scotland. A toddy iron would be used to stir the liquid to keep it hot.

Rum was a major import from the Carribean, and it became one of the imports that became difficult to get during the Revolutionary War.

The following recipe is based on John Adams's description in the "Account of the Manner of Life of the different Ranks of the Inhabitants of America," published in *The Weekly Entertainer* in 1784: "…between twelve and one, he takes a draught of bombo, or toddy, a liquor composed of water, sugar, rum, and nutmeg, which is made weak, and kept cool."

2 tablespoons rum
¾ cup lukewarm water
2 teaspoons brown sugar or molasses
nutmeg

In an 8-ounce cup or glass, mix the rum and water. Stir in the sugar, to taste.

Add a pinch of nutmeg.

Abigail visited her daughter, Nabby, in Eastchester, New York, in July of 1797. From there, she wrote a letter to her sister Mary Smith Cranch, instructing her how to prepare punch back in Braintree, as Abigail would not be able to return until mid-October.

> I must beg of you to make such arrangments of punch & wine as may be necessary… Wine you can draw from the casks in the cellar. Punch must be made by Gallons. You will procure spirit for the purpose, and in a Box in the North cellar which is naild up is some Jamaca spirit, that with some Brandy will answer.[15]

In John Adams's time, punch was a gentlemen's drink, served at social gatherings, special occasions, and celebrations. The punch bowl was one of the most valuable items in a household.

Abigail also told Mary about punch served for the Fourth of July in Philadelphia.

> I got through the 4 July with much more ease than I expected. It was a fine cool day, and my fatigue arose chiefly from being drest at an early hour, and receiving the very numerous sets of company who were so polite as to pay their compliments to me in succession in my drawing Room after visiting the President below, and partaking of cake, wine & punch with him.[16]

John wrote to Abigail on January 1, 1799, about some celebratory punch-drinking:

> We have had more Company to Day than ever upon any Occasion. Thirty or forty Gallons of Punch, Wine in Proportion: and Cake in Abundance. The News by The America Captn. Jenkins arrived at Newbury Port made every body gay…[17]

Photo by Ed Nute

The English painter William Hogarth (1697-1764) captured the place of punch in society in his 1732 painting *A Midnight Modern Conversation*. Hogarth shows a group of aristocratic men gathered around a table. They have drunk a little too much from the punch bowl.

This recipe is based on Abigail's instructions to Mary.

Makes 3 ½ quarts (14 cups)

    2 oranges, sliced
    2 lemons, sliced
    Juice of 12 to 16 medium oranges (about 5 cups), or 5 cups prepared orange juice, with or without pulp.
    Juice of 12 to 15 medium lemons (about 3 cups), or 3 cups prepared juice
    1 cup brandy
    1 cup rum
    Approximately 1 cup sugar
    3 cups water
    ice cubes or one block of ice

Slice the oranges and lemons and place in a large mixing bowl or punch bowl. If you prefer to use only the rind, remove the bitter white inner lining before slicing the peel.

Pour the juices into the mixing bowl.

Add the brandy and rum. Add sugar, to taste, and dilute with water to your preference.

The punch can be strained through a jelly bag, clean pillowcase, or a double layer of cheesecloth to remove any pulp.

Add the ice before serving to keep the punch cold. Ladle into small drinking glasses or punch cups to serve. The punch can be stored in a sealable jug.

William Hogarth's *A Midnight Modern Conversation*, 1732. *Courtesy of Yale Center for British Art, Paul Mellon Collection*

In the early eighteenth century, British Royal Navy Vice-Admiral Edward Vernon, known as "Old Grog," because of the wool grogram coat he often wore, suggested adding some lemon juice and water to the rum on his ship, to decrease the amount of alcohol his men were drinking and to prevent them from becoming drunk. Soon he found that his men were healthier than the men on other naval ships.

The drink became known as "grog" in honor of its creator.

John Adams first mentioned grog in his diary when boarding an American frigate to Europe.

> TUESDAY NOVR.18 1777... Lodged at Brooks's, 5 Miles from the North River. Rode to the Continental Ferry, crossed over, and dined at Fish Kill, at the Drs. Mess, near the Hospital, with Dr. Sam. Adams, Dr. Eustis, Mr. Wells, &c. It was a feast—Salt Pork and Cabbage, roast Beef and Potatoes, and a noble suit Pudding, Grog and a Glass of Port.[18]

The following recipe is based on a description published in the *Gentleman's Magazine and Historical Chronicle*, Volume 40 (1770): "Groggy; this is a West-Indian Phrase; Rum and Water, without sugar, being called Grogg."

2 ounces dark rum
1 cup water
Lemon juice, to taste

Mix the rum and water in a cup. Add lemon juice, as desired.

A Note on Taverns

In his early years as a colonist, John Adams opposed the idea of public houses and taverns where they served beer and ale. As a student at Harvard College he witnessed many young people wasting their fortunes in these houses and being fined for playing cards, tardiness and other matters.[19]

He once drew up a map showing the locations of all the local taverns.

But by the time he went to Philadelphia as a delegate in 1774, his anti-tavern stance had abated. He witnessed how taverns served as political outposts. Some changed their names to show their support for the war. On August 25, 1774, while on the way to Philadelphia for the First Continental Congress, John and the Massachusetts delegates stopped in New York to attend a gathering hosted by New York delegates at Fraunces Tavern (formerly known as Queen's Head Tavern).[20] John recalled that night: "We afterwards dined in the Exchange Chamber, at the Invitation of the Committee of Correspondence, with more than 50 Gentlemen, at the most splendid Dinner I ever saw—a Profusion of rich Dishes..."[21]

It was in these places that revolutionary groups could discuss and exchange ideas. Newspapers and mail were delivered here, and people sought news and gossip at their local taverns. In 1776, Thomas Paine's book *Common Sense* was popular reading material in taverns.

General George Washington gave his farewell address and resigned as the commander in chief of the Continental Army at Fraunces Tavern. As President, he hosted balls at the tavern. After the capital was moved to New York in 1785, Fraunces Tavern became a major place to conduct political gatherings and business. The department of the Treasury and Secretary of War had offices there.

Because they traveled frequently to New York, Philadelphia, and then Washington City, John and Abigail had a list of taverns where they'd regularly spend a night. Some, like Widow Haviland's Tavern in Rye, New York, later became museums. Others still operate as taverns, including Fraunces Tavern in New York, City Tavern in Philadelphia, and Gadsby Tavern in Alexandria, Virginia.

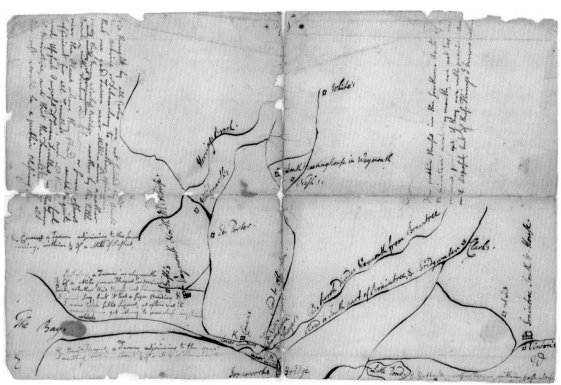

John was fascinated by the growing number of taverns in the Massachusetts towns of Braintree and Weymouth. In 1761, after voting in favor of them, he sketched this map and listed the number of such taverns or "licensed houses." Manuscript map of taverns in Braintree and Weymouth, Mass. Pen and ink by John Adams, circa 1760. Original manuscript from Adams All Generations. Massachusetts Historical Society. *Courtesy of The Massachusetts Historical Society, Boston, Massachusetts.*

CHAPTER 11

Bills of Fare

While his critics accused John Adams of being a monarchist, both John and Abigail did not enjoy formal dinner settings but preferred the frugal lifestyle of their New England roots. However, when they were in Europe, the couple attended many elegant dinner parties while Adams served in his role as the first Ambassador to the Court of St. James in Great Britain.

When John Adams took office as the president in 1797, Abigail Adams adopted some of the formal dining customs introduced by her predecessor, First Lady Martha Washington. Among them was the practice of sending out invitation cards, like the one below, which can found at the Massachusetts Historical Society.

Many cookbooks of the Adamses' time included instructions on how to lay food out on a dining table according to the availability of food products throughout the year. Some books included illustrations.

According to these sources, and depending on the occasion, a meal usually consisted of three courses.

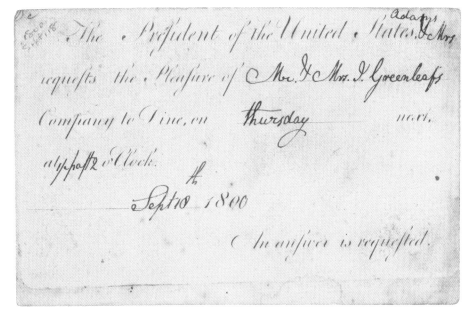

A dinner invitation card from President John and Abigail Adams to Mr. & Mrs. Greenleaf, 18 September 1800. *Original manuscript from Miscellaneous Manuscripts. Massachusetts Historical Society.*

The Adams family might have followed ideas found in sources like Martha Bradley's *The British Housewife: or the Cook, Housekeeper's and Gardiner's Companion* (1770 edition). This guide offered advice on everything from serving meals to home remedies for treating minor illnesses.

These templates of table set-ups give a sense of what John and Abigail experienced and used in formal engagements. It is worth noting that the Adamses did not own slaves, but instead hired help when they were in Washington. Before Adams left Washington, he wrote: "I have always employed freemen, both domestics and laborers, and never in my life did I own a slave."[1]

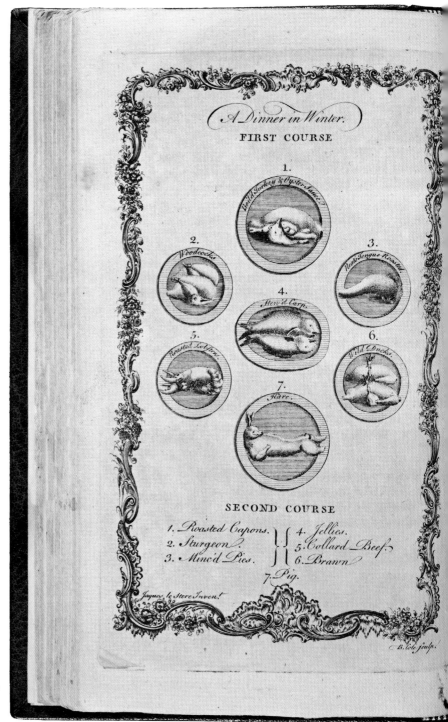

"A Dinner in Winter" from Martha Bradley's *The British Housewife*, 1770. *Courtesy of The Colonial Williamsburg Foundation.*

On some grand occasions, such as a wedding, the number of dishes presented at the table increased, as shown in this image from Martha Bradley's book.

In his retirement, John Adams wrote to Dr. Benjamin Rush, on Christmas Day 1811: "I dined a large company once or twice a week. Jefferson dined a dozen every day."[2]

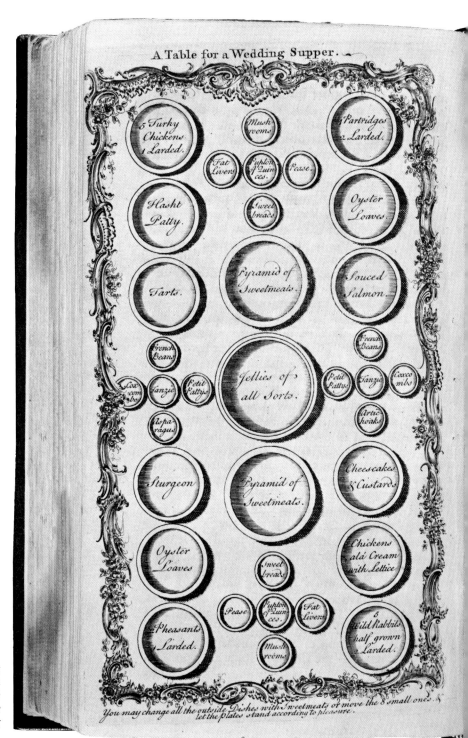

"A Table for a Wedding Supper" from Martha Bradley's *The British Housewife*, 1770. *Courtesy of The Colonial Williamsburg Foundation.*

Epilogue

Throughout the fifty-four years of their marriage, John and Abigail Adams shared their love of life through sacrifice, duty, and the pursuit of happiness for their family and for the founding a new nation. They shared their thoughts and dreams through letters that preserve these notions for future generations.

Food was a part of their personal stories and a part of the story of their times.

The series of taxes that the British Parliament imposed on the colonies mainly concerned food. Tea! Sugar! The colonists, in response, turned to other staples to meet their needs, like coffee, whisky, and cider.

While the couple corresponded about governmental affairs and the dawn of democracy in America, they also wrote about cooking and bread baking and gardening. These daily tasks were affected by the politics of revolution and then by independence.

The mahogany dining table at Peace field is American-made, circa 1760-1780. *Courtesy of the National Park Service, Adams National Historic Park.*

Even though they found the grand European lifestyle fascinating, they preferred their home in the New World. In 1783, Abigail wrote to John:

> I had much rather see you in America, than Europe. I well know that real true and substantial happiness depend not upon titles Rank and fortune; the Gay coach, the Brilliant attire; the pomp and Etiquet of Courts; rob, the mind of that placid harmony, that social intercourse which is an Enemy to ceremony. [2]

And just as they preferred the egalitarian nature of the colonies, they also preferred its food culture, which called for more simple meals, eating without excess, and eating equally. As America developed its sense of independence, it also developed its own cuisine.

In 1796, *American Cookery* was published. It was the first cookbook written by an American and published in the United States. The author, Amelia Simmons, called herself an "American orphan." This cookbook not only gave tips for housewives on how to cook, but also helped create a sense of identity in the new nation. Simmons' cookbook addressed the common man (or woman) and defined America as a place with a unique food culture.

While the Adamses wrote about food in their personal correspondence, there was a broader dialogue going on in the world of food as ideas went back and forth between the Old and New Worlds. During the late 1700s, European cookbooks began to include some of the staple food items indigenous to the Americas, such as chocolate, turkey, and corn.

In their retirement, John and Abigail Adams enjoyed their home at Peace field in Quincy, Massachusetts, more than ever with their extended family. After Abigail's death in 1818, John continued to share his love of food and life at Peace field.

During the day, alone at his desk in the study on the second floor, Adams continued to write letters. Some were to Thomas Jefferson. While they had stopped communicating when Adams lost the presidency to Jefferson in 1800, in 1812, Dr. Benjamin Rush had reunited the two former friends.

The two patriots continued to share their dreams and ideas.

Jefferson once famously said, "I like the dreams of the future more than the history of the past," and it is interesting to think about how these two men would have reacted to the progress in America's food culture, the revolutions in food processing, preparation, cooking and nutrition.

Progess and education were fundamental ideas that Adams and Jefferson fought for in the founding of this nation, and today we continue to educate ourselves about food, focusing now on nutrition, healthy habits, and even a return to nonprocessed whole foods such as the ones enjoyed by John and Abigail Adams.

John Adams, we can imagine, would probably not have been terribly surprised by America's progress in the development of its food culture. After all, he had observed how particularly interested in food the people of his own times were.

In a letter to Elias Boudinot, he wrote:

> A Bookseller in London gave me the Character of this Age, in part by an Account of the Trade in Books, of Hannah Glass's Cookery, they sold Thirteen thousand Copies a year. Of the Pilgrims Progress two thousand, of the whole Duty of Man Eight Thousand, from these pacts he inferred that gluttony was the first, supensth then the seem and a rational Piety the third Ingredient in the Character of the Age. [2]

And so the love of food crosses the boundaries of time, connecting us with with our past and also with our future.

Notes

Introduction

1. Kaminski, John P., Ed. *The Quotable Abigail Adams.*(Cambridge: Belknap Press of Harvard University Press. 2009), 314.

Author's note: The idea of a day of thanksgiving was passed down from the Pilgrims at the Plymouth Plantation, but it was not until December 26, 1941, that President Franklin D. Roosevelt signed the resolution that the federal holiday would be celebrated on the last Thursday of November. In John Adams's time, the exact days of thanksgiving varied.

2. Adams, Abigail. Abigail Adams to John Adams, October 25 1782. [electronic edition] The Adams Papers Digital Edition, ed. C. James Taylor. (Boston: Massachusetts Historical Society, 2007.) http://www.masshist.org/ff/

3. Adams, John Letter from John Adams to Abigail Adams, 14 April 1797. [electronic edition] The Adams Papers Digital Edition, ed. C. James Taylor. (Boston: Massachusetts Historical Society, 2007.) http://www.masshist. org/ff/

4. Adams, Abigail. Abigail Adams to John Adams, 22 October 1775. [electronic edition] The Adams Papers Digital Edition, ed. C. James Taylor. (Boston: Massachusetts Historical Society, 2007.) http://www.masshist.org/ff/

5. Adams, John. Diary of John Adams, Summer 1759 [electronic edition] The Adams Papers Digital Edition, ed. C. James Taylor. (Boston: Massachusetts Historical Society, 2007.) http://www.masshist.org/ff/

6. Adams, Joh. Letter to Abigail Adams, 13 February 1779. [elenctronic edition}. *A*dams Family Papers: An Electronic Archive. Massachusetts Historical Society. http://www.masshist.org/digitaladams/

7. Adams, Abigail. Letter to John Adams, 7 May 1783 [electronic edition]. Adams Family Papers: An Electronic Archive. Massachusetts Historical Society. http://www.masshist.org/ digitaladams

8. Mitchell, Stewart, Ed. *New Letters of Abigail Adams: 1788-1801.* (New York: Houghton & Mifflin, 1947), 91.

9. Adams, John. Letter to Abigail Adams, 19 December 1793 [electronic edition]. Adams Family Papers: An Electronic Archive. Massachusetts Historical Society. http://www. masshist.org/digitaladams/

10. Adams, John. Letter to Abigail Adams, 17 February 1793. [electronic edition]. *A*dams Family Papers: An Electronic Archive. Massachusetts Historical Society. http://www.masshist.org/ digitaladams/

11. Abigail Adams. Letter to John Adams, 8-10 September 1775 [electronic edition]. Adams Family Papers: An Electronic Archive. Massachusetts Historical Society. http://www. masshist.org/digitaladams

12. Adams, Abigail. Letter from Abigail Adams to John Adams, 21 October 1775. [electronic edition] The Adams Papers Digital Edition, ed. C. James Taylor. (Boston: Massachusetts Historical Society, 2007.) http:// www.masshist.org/ff/

13. Adams, Abigail. Letter to John Adams, 5 July 1775. [electronic edition]. *A*dams Family Papers: An Electronic Archive. Massachusetts Historical Society. http://www.masshist.org/ digitaladams/

14. Adams, Abigail. Letter to John Adams, 5 July 1775. [electronic edition]. Adams Family Papers: An Electronic Archive. Massachusetts Historical Society. http://www.masshist.org/ digitaladams/

15. Adams, Abigail. Letter to John Adams, 16 July 1775. [electronic edition]. Adams Family Papers: An Electronic Archive. Massachusetts Historical Society. http://www.masshist.org/ digitaladams/

16. Adams, Abigail. Letter to John Adams, 27 November 1775. [electronic edition]. Adams Family Papers: An Electronic Archive. Massachusetts Historical Society. http://www.masshist.org/digitaladams/

17. Eaton, Mary. *The Cook and Housekeeper's Complete and Universal Dictionary*. (Bungay: Printed and Published by J. and R. Childs. 1823.), x-xi.

18. Adams, Abigail. Letter to John Adams. 28 December 1798.[electronic edition]. Adams Family Papers: An Electronic Archive. Massachusetts Historical Society. http://www.masshist.org/ff/

Chapter 1: Breakfast

1. Adams, John. Diary of John Adams 22 August 1774. [electronic edition] The Adams Papers Digital Edition, ed. C. James Taylor. (Boston: Massachusetts Historical Society, 2007.) http://www.masshist.org/ff

2. Adams, John. Letter to Abigail Adams, 17 July 1775. [electronic edition] The Adams Papers Digital Edition, ed. C. James Taylor. (Boston: Massachusetts Historical Society, 2007.) http://www.masshist.org/ff

3. Adams, John. Diary of John Adams, 23 July 1771. [electronic edition] The Adams Papers Digital Edition, ed. C. James Taylor. (Boston: Massachusetts Historical Society, 2007.) http://www.masshist.org/ff

4. Adams, John. Letter to Abigail Adams, 11 August 1777. [electronic edition] The Adams Papers Digital Edition, ed. C. James Taylor. (Boston: Massachusetts Historical Society, 2007.) http://www.masshist.org/ff/

5. Adams, John. Letter to Abigail Adams, 11 August 1777. [electronic edition] The Adams Papers Digital Edition, ed. C. James Taylor. (Boston: Massachusetts Historical Society, 2007.) http://www.masshist.org/ff/

6. Adams, John Quincy. Diary of John Quincy Adams, 28 July 1780. John Quincy Adams diary 3, 25 July 1780 - 30 September 1780, page 2 [electronic edition]. *The Diaries of John Quincy Adams: A Digital Collection.* Boston, Mass. : Massachusetts Historical Society, 2005. http://www.masshist.org/jqadiaries

7. Adams, John. Diary of John Adams, 18 June 1779 [electronic edition] The Adams Papers Digital Edition, ed. C. James Taylor. (Boston: Massachusetts Historical Society, 2007.) http://www.masshist.org/ff/

8. Adams, John. Diary of John Adams, 10 December 1779. [electronic edition] The Adams Papers Digital Edition, ed. C. James Taylor. (Boston: Massachusetts Historical Society, 2007.) http://www.masshist.org/ff/

9. Adams, John. Letter to John Quincy Adams, 28 May 1784. [electronic edition] The Adams Papers Digital Edition, ed. C. James Taylor. (Boston: Massachusetts Historical Society, 2007.) http://www.masshist.org/ff/

10. Adams, John. Diary of John Adams, 7 June 1771. [electronic edition] The Adams Papers Digital Edition, ed. C. James Taylor. (Boston: Massachusetts Historical Society, 2007.) http://www.masshist.org/ff

11. Adams, Abigail. Letter from Abigail Adams to John Adams, 28 November 1793. 4 pages. Original manuscript from the Adams Family Papers, Massachusetts Historical Society.

12. Adams, Abigail. Letter to John Adams, 22 August 1777. [electronic edition]*Founding Families Digital Editions: Papers of the Winthrops and Adamses*, (Boston: Massachusetts Historical Society.) http://www.masshist.org/ff/

13. Adams, Abigail. *Letter from Abigail Adams to John Adams, 27 December 1783*. 4 pages. Original manuscript from the Adams Family Papers, Massachusetts Historical Society.

14. Adams, John. Letter to Abigail Adams, 6 August 1777. [electronic edition] The Adams Papers Digital Edition, ed. C. James Taylor. (Boston: Massachusetts Historical Society, 2007.) http://www.masshist.org/ff

15. Adams, John. Diary of John Adams, 30 December 1779. [electronic edition] The Adams Papers Digital Edition, ed. C. James Taylor. (Boston: Massachusetts Historical Society, 2007.) http://www.masshist.org/ff/

16. Adams, Abigail. Letter to John Adams, 20 April 1777. [electronic edition] The Adams Papers Digital Edition, ed. C. James Taylor. (Boston: Massachusetts Historical Society, 2007.) http://www.masshist.org/ff/

17. Adams, Abigail. Letter from Abigail Adams to John Adams, 20 March-23 April 1779, with one enclosure. 5 pages. Original manuscript from the Adams Family Papers, Massachusetts Historical Society.

18. Adams, Abigail. Letter from Abigail Adams to John Adams, 3 November 1789 [electronic edition]. Adams Family Papers: An Electronic Archive. Massachusetts Historical Society. http://www.masshist.org/digitaladams/

19. Oliver, Sandra L. *Food in Colonial and Federal America.* (Westport: Greenwood Press. 2005.), 42.

20. Adams, John. Diary of John Adams, 1774 September 21. Wednesday. [electronic edition] The Adams Papers Digital Edition, ed. C. James Taylor. (Boston: Massachusetts Historical Society, 2007.) http://www.masshist.org/ff/

21. Adams, John. Diary of John Adams, 15 January 1766. [electronic edition]. Adams Family Papers: An Electronic Archive. Massachusetts Historical Society. http://www.masshist.org/ff/

22. Adams, Abigail. Letter to John Adams. 21 October 1775. [electronic edition]. Adams Family Papers: An Electronic Archive. Massachusetts Historical Society. http://www.masshist.org/ff/

23. Rundell, Maria Eliza Ketelby. *A New System of domestic cookery: formed upon principles of economy, and adapted to the use of private families throughout the United States.* (New York: R. M'Dermut and D.D. Arden. 1814.), 272.

24. Adams, John. Diary: 21 September 1774. Wednesday. [electronic edition] *A*dams Electronic Archive. Boston: Massachusetts Historical Society. http://www.masshist.org/digitaladams/

25. Adams, John. Letter to Abigail Adams Smith. 12 December 1772. [electronic edition] The Adams Papers Digital Edition, ed. C. James Taylor. (Boston: Massachusetts Historical Society, 2007.) http://www.masshist.org/ff/

26. Adams, John. Diary of John Adams, 13 November 1779-6 January 1780 [electronic edition]. *Adams Family Papers: An Electronic Archive.* Massachusetts Historical Society. http://www.masshist.org/digitaladams/

27. Colmenero de Ledesma, Antonio. Chocolate: or, An Indian Drinke. Translated by Capt. James Wadsworth, London: Printed by J.G. for Iohn Dakins 1652. www.gutenberg.org

28. Adams, Abigail. Letter to John Adams, 19 April 1794. [electronic edition]. Adams Family Papers: An Electronic Archive. Massachusetts Historical Society. http://www.masshist.org/digitaladams/

29. Mitchell, Stewart, Ed. *New Letters of Abigail Adams: 1788-1801.* (New York: Houghton & Mifflin,1947), 141.

Chapter 2: Bread

1. Oliver, Sandra L. *Food in Colonial and Federal America.* (Westport: Greenwood Press. 2005.), 41.

2. Adams, John. John Adams autobiography, part 1, "John Adams," through 1776, sheet 44 of 53 [electronic edition]. Adams Family Papers: An Electronic Archive. Massachusetts Historical Society. http://www.masshist.org/digitaladams/

3. Adams, John. John Adams diary 17, 16 April-14 June 1771 [electronic edition]. Adams Family Papers: An Electronic Archive. Massachusetts Historical Society. http://www.masshist.org/digitaladams/

4. Adams, Abigail. Letter from Abigail Adams to John Adams, 29 September 1778, draft. Letter from Abigail Adams to John Adams, 29 September 1778, draft [electronic edition]. Adams Family Papers: An Electronic Archive. Massachusetts Historical Society. http://www.masshist.org/digitaladams//

5. De Windt, Caroline Amelia Smith, Ed. *Journal and Correspondence of Miss Adams, Daughter of John Adams, Second President of the United States.* Written in France and England, in 1785., Volume 1. (New York: Wiley and Putnam. 1841.), 221-224.

6. Mitchell, Stewart, Ed. *New Letters of Abigail Adams: 1788-1801.* (New York: Houghton & Mifflin Co. 1947.), 149.

7. Adams, John. Diary of John Adams, 30 June 1770. [electronic edition] The Adams Papers Digital Edition, ed. C. James Taylor. (Boston: Massachusetts Historical Society, 2007.) http://www.masshist.org/ff/

8. Richards, Laura Elizabeth Howe. *Abigail Adams and her Times.* (New York: D. Appleton and Company, 1917.), 264-265.

9. Parkinson, Richard. *Tour in America in 1798, 1799, and 1800: Exhibiting Sketches of Society and Manners, and A Particular Account of the American System of Agriculture, with its Recent Improvements, Volume 2.* (Printed for J. Harding, St. James's Street; and J Murray, Fleet Street. 1805), 631-632

Chapter 3: Meat and Poultry

1. Adams, John. Diary of John Adams, 25 June 1760. John Adams diary 5, 26 May - 25 November 1760 [electronic edition]. Adams Family Papers: An Electronic Archive. Massachusetts Historical Society. http://www.masshist.org/digitaladams/

2. Adams, John. John Adams autobiography, part 3, *"Peace," 1777-1778.* Part 3 is comprised of 18 sheets and 1 insertion; 72 pages total. Original manuscript from the Adams Family Papers, Massachusetts Historical Society.

3. Adams the 2nd, Abigail. Abigail Adams 2nd to John Quincy Adams, 24 September 1785. [electronic edition] The Adams Papers Digital Edition, ed. C. James Taylor (Boston: Massachusetts Historical Society, 2007.) http://www.masshist.org/ff/

4. Adams, John. Letter from John Adams to Abigail Adams, 9 July 1774. [electronic edition]. Adams Family Papers: An Electronic Archive. Massachusetts Historical Society. http://www.masshist.org/digitaladams/

5. Adams, John. Diary of John Adams. 30 December 1779. [electronic edition] The Adams Papers Digital Edition, ed. C. James Taylor. (Boston: Massachusetts Historical Society, 2007.) http://www.masshist.org/ff/

6. Letter from Abigail Adams to John Adams, 16, January 1795 [electronic edition]. Adams Family Papers: An Electronic Archive. Massachusetts Historical Society. http://www.masshist.org/digitaladams/

7. Adams, John. Diary of John Adams, Monday. Nov. 17. 1777. [electronic edition] The Adams Papers Digital Edition, ed. C. James Taylor. (Boston: Massachusetts Historical Society, 2007.) http://www.masshist.org/ff/

8. Adams, John. John Adams Letterbook: Letter to François Adriaan van der Kemp. 23 February 1815. Adams Family Papers, Reel #122. (Quincy: Adams National Historical Park)

9. Adams, John. Diary 28, 6 February - 21 November 1777 [electronic edition]. Adams Family Papers: An Electronic Archive. Massachusetts Historical Society. http://www.masshist.org/digitaladams/

10. Adams, John. Letter from John Adams to Abigail Adams, 31 August 1782 [electronic edition], Adams Family Papers: An Electronic Archive, Massa chusetts Historical Society. http://www.masshist.org/digitaladams/

11. Adams, Abigail. Abigail Adams Diary: "Voyage from America to England 1784", 25 July1784. [electronic edition] The Adams Papers Digital Edition, ed. C. James Taylor. (Boston: Massachusetts Historical Society, 2007.) http://www.masshist.org/ff/

12. Adams, Abigail. Abigail Adams Diary: "Voyage from America to England 1784", 25 July1784. [electronic edition] The Adams Papers Digital Edition, ed. C. James Taylor. (Boston: Massachusetts Historical Society, 2007.) http://www.masshist.org/ff/

13. Adams, Abigail. Abigail Adams to Mary Smith Cranch, 19 June 1789. [electronic edition] The Adams Papers Digital Edition, ed. C. James Taylor (Boston: Massachusetts Historical Society, 2007.) http://www.masshist.org/ff/

14. Adams, John. Diary of John Adams. 31 March 1778 [electronic edition]. The Adams Papers Digital Edition, ed. C. James Taylor (Boston: Massachusetts Historical Society, 2007.) http:// www.masshist.org/ff/

15. Do not confuse this type of bouilli with another definition of the term. In *Mastering the Art of French Cooking*, Julia Child defines bouillie as a sauce base for making desserts. "A bouillie is milk, sugar, and flour or starch, boiled for a few seconds until thickened. After it has cooled slightly, egg yolks, butter, and flavoring are beaten in, then beaten egg whites are incorporated. Some people prefer a bouillie with flour; other use potato starch, rice starch, or corn starch." Child: Vol. 1, 614.

16. Anonymous. *French Domestic Cookery, by an English Physician.* London: Printed for Thomas Boys, 7, Ludgate-Hill. 1825), 39-40.

17. Adams, John. Autobiography, part 3, "Peace," 1779-1780, sheet 6 of 18 [electronic edition]. Adams Family Papers: An Electronic Archive. Massachusetts Historical Society. http://www.masshist.org/digitaladams/

18. Simmons, Amelia. *The First American Cookbook, A Facsimile of "American Cookery" 1796.* With an Essay by Mary Tolford Wilson. (New York: Dover Publications, Inc. 1984.), 18.

19. Adams, John. Diary of John Adams, 7 September 1774. [electronic edition] The Adams Papers Digital Edition, ed. C. James Taylor. (Boston: Massachusetts Historical Society, 2007.) http://www.masshist.org/ff/

Chapter 4: Sauces

1. Adams, John. Diary of John Adams 8 April 1767. [electronic edition] The Adams Papers Digital Edition, ed. C. James Taylor. (Boston: Massachusetts Historical Society, 2007.) http://www.masshist.org/ff/

2. Hess, Karen. *The Virginia House-Wife by Mary Randolph, with Historical Notes and Commentaries.* (Columbia: University of South Carolina Press. 1984.).,xvi

3. Tudor, William. *Miscellenous* (Boston: Wells and Lily, 1821.), 22

4. Adams, Abigail. Letter to John Adams, 22 August, 1777. [electronic edition] The Adams Papers Digital Edition, ed. C. James Taylor. (Boston: Massachusetts Historical Society, 2007.) http://www.masshist.org/ff/

Chapter 5: Seafood

1. Anonymous. *Cookery Reformed; Or the Lady's Assistant.* (London: Printed by P. Davey and B. Law. 1755.), 53.

2. Adams, Abigail. Letter to Mary Smith Cranch. 28 July 1784. . [electronic edition] The Adams Papers Digital Edition, ed. C. James Taylor. (Boston: Massachusetts Historical Society, 2007.) http://www.masshist.org/ff/82

3. Carter, Susannah. *The Frugal Housewife or Complete woman cook.* (Philadelphia: James Carey), 49.

4. Adams, John. Letter to Abigail Smith. 4 May 1764. [electronic edition]. Adams Family Papers: An Electronic Archive. Massachusetts Historical Society. http://www.masshist.org/digitaladams/

5. Adams, John. Adams' Argument for the Defense: 3-4 December 1770. Legal Papers of John Adams, Volume 3. [electronic edition] The Adams Papers Digital Edition, ed. C. James Taylor. (Boston: Massachusetts Historical Society, 2007.) http://www.masshist.org/ff/

6. Adams, John. Autobiography , 14 December 1779. [electronic edition] The Adams Papers Digital Edition, ed. C. James Taylor. (Boston: Massachusetts Historical Society, 2007.) http://www.masshist.org/ff/

7. Adams, Abigail. Letter to John Adams. 16 November 1798. [electronic edition]. Adams Family Papers: An Electronic Archive. Massachusetts Historical Society. http://www.masshist.org/digitaladams/

8. Adams, John. Letter to Abigail Adams, 16 January 1797 [electronic edition]. Adams Family Papers: An Electronic Archive. Massachusetts Historical Society. http://www.masshist.org/digitaladams/

9. Adams, John. Letter to Abigail Adams, 16 January 1797 [electronic edition]. Adams Family Papers: An Electronic Archive. Massachusetts Historical Society. http://www.masshist.org/digitaladams/

10. Adams, Abigail. Letter from Abigail Adams to John Adams, 7 May 1783. [electronic edition]. *Adams Family Papers: An Electronic Archive.* Massachusetts Historical Society. http://www.masshist.org/digitaladams/

11. Adams, Abigail. Letter to John Adams, 25 October 1789. [Electronic edition]. Adams Family Papers: An Electronic Archive. Massachusetts Historical Society. http://www.masshist.org/digitaladams/

12. Allison, Robert J. *A Short History of Cape Cod.* (Beverly: Commonwealth Editions. 2010.), 24.

13. Cranch, Richard. Letter to John Adams, 26 June 1783. [electronic edition] The Adams Papers Digital Edition, ed. C. James Taylor. (Boston: Massachusetts Historical Society, 2007.) http://www.masshist.org/ff/

14. Adams, John. Letter to Richard Cranch, 10 September 1783 [electronic edition] The Adams Papers Digital Edition, ed. C. James Taylor. (Boston: Massachusetts Historical Society, 2007.) http://www.masshist.org/ff/

15. Adams, John. Letter to Richard Cranch, Paris, 15 December 1782. [electronic edition] The Adams Papers Digital Edition, ed. C. James Taylor. (Boston: Massachusetts Historical Society, 2007.) http://www.masshist.org/ff/

16. From the footnotes by the Massachusetts Historical Society's webpage, MHS Digital Editions: Adams Papers

17. Corson, Trevor. *The Secret Life of Lobsters.* (New York: Harpers Collins 2009.), 26

Chapter 6: Vegetables

1. Adams, John. Letter to Abigail Adams, 24 June 1795 [electronic edition]. Adams Family Papers: An Electronic Archive. Massachusetts Historical Society. http://www.masshist.org/digitaladams/

2. Adams, John. Diary of John Adams, 4 January 1780. [electronic edition] The Adams Papers Digital Edition, ed. C. James Taylor. (Boston: Massachusetts Historical Society, 2007.) http://www.masshist.org/ff/

3. Adams, John. John Adams diary 42, 14 September-27 October 1783 [electronic edition]. Adams Family Papers: An Electronic Archive. Massachusetts Historical Society. http://www.masshist.org/digitaladams/

4. Adams, Abigail. Abigail Adams to Isaac Smith, Sr., 8 May 1785. [electronic edition] The Adams Papers Digital Edition, ed. C. James Taylor (Boston: Massachusetts Historical Society, 2007.) http://www.masshist.org/ff/

5. Adams, Abigail. Letter to Mary Smith Cranch, 12 September 1786. [electronic edition] The Adams Papers Digital Edition, ed. C. James Taylor (Boston: Massachusetts Historical Society, 2007.) http://www.masshist.org/ff/

6. Adams, John. Letter to Abigail Adams, 13 May 1789 [electronic edition]. Adams Family Papers: An Electronic Archive. Massachusetts Historical Society. http://www.masshist.org/digitaladams/

7. Adams, Abigail. Letter to John Adams, 25 June 1795 [electronic edition]. Adams Family Papers: An Electronic Archive. Massachusetts Historical Society. http://www.masshist.org/digitaladams/

8. Adams, Abigail. Letter to John Adams, 10 November 1789 [electronic edition]. Adams Family Papers: An Electronic Archive. Massachusetts Historical Society. http://www.masshist.org/digitaladams/

9. Adams, Abigail. Letter to John Adams, 25 June 1795 [electronic edition]. Adams Family Papers: An Electronic Archive. Massachusetts Historical Society. http://www.masshist.org/digitaladams/

10. Adams, John. Letter to Abigail Adams, 11 March 1794 [electronic edition]. Adams Family Papers: An Electronic Archive. Massachusetts Historical Society. http://www.masshist.org/digitaladams/

11. Adams, Abigail. Letter to John Adams, 4 February 1799 [electronic edition]. Adams Family Papers: An Electronic Archive. Massachusetts Historical Society. http://www.masshist.org/digitaladams/

12. Adams, John. Diary of John Adams: 24 August 1796. John Adams diary 46, 6 August 1787 - 10 September 1796, 2 July - 21 August 1804. Grouping of 9 fragments of loose and/or folded sheets (65 pages and additional blank pages). Original manuscript from the Adams Family Papers, Massachusetts Historical Society.

13. Duffy, John. *From Humors to Medical Science: A History of American Medicine.* (Chicago: University of Illinois Press: 1993), 80.

14. Adams, Abigail. Letter to John Adams, 20 October 1799 [electronic edition]. Adams Family Papers: An Electronic Archive. Massachusetts Historical Society. http://www.masshist.org/digitaladams/

15. Adams, John. Letter to Abigail Adams. 29 June 1774. [electronic edition]. Adams Family Papers: An Electronic Archive. Massachusetts Historical Society. http://www.masshist.org/digitaladams/

16. Adams, Abigail. Letter from Abigail Adams to John Adams, 31 May 1789. [electronic edition]. *Adams Family Papers: An Electronic Archive.* Massachusetts Historical Society. http://www.masshist.org/digitaladams/

17. Adams, John. Letter to Abigail Adams, 9 July 1774 [electronic edition]. Adams Family Papers: An Electronic Archive. Massachusetts Historical Society. http://www.masshist.org/digitaladams/

18. Adams, John. Letter to Abigail Adams, 2 - 3 August 1777 [electronic edition] The Adams Papers Digital Edition, ed. C. James Taylor. (Boston: Massachusetts Historical Society, 2007.) http://www.masshist.org/ff

19. Adams, Abigail. Letter to John Adams: 29 September 1776. [electronic edition] The Adams Papers Digital Edition, ed. C. James Taylor. (Boston: Massachusetts Historical Society, 2007.) http://www.masshist.org/ff/

20 Adams, John. John Adams diary: 1 April 1778. [electronic edition] The Adams Papers Digital Edition, ed. C. James Taylor. (Boston: Massachusetts Historical Society, 2007.) http://www.masshist.org/ff/

21. *A Boiled Salad, Second Lesson. Foodways: My So-Called Pilgrim Life.* Plimoth Plantation. http://blogs.plimoth.org/village/?cat=7

22. Lawson, John. *A New Voyage to Carolina*, (London. 1709.), 77

23. Adams, John. Letter to Abigail Adams 1 July 1774. [electronic edition] The Adams Papers Digital Edition, ed. C. James Taylor. (Boston: Massachusetts Historical Society, 2007.) http://www.masshist.org/ff/

24. Adams, John. Letter to Cotton Tufts: 9 April 1764. [electronic edition] The Adams Papers Digital Edition, ed. C. James Taylor. (Boston: Massachusetts Historical Society, 2007.) http://www.masshist.org/ff/

25. Collingwood, Francis & John Wollams. *The Universal Cook and City and Country Housekeeper.* (London: Printed by R. Noble, for J. Scatcherd and J. Whitaker.), 209.

26. Allison, Robert J. *A Short History of Cape Cod.* (Beverly: Commonwealth Edition.2010). 29-31

27. Popularly known as Pilgrims. One of John Adams's ancestors was John Alden, who was one of the leaders of this group that migrated to the New World.

28. Benjamin Franklin: *Writings.* (New York: Literary Classics of the United States. Library of America. 1987.), 568

29. Adams, John. Diary of John Adams, 14 July 1796. [electronic edition] The Adams Papers Digital Edition, ed. C. James Taylor. (Boston: Massachusetts Historical Society, 2007.) http://www.masshist.org/ff/

Chapter 7: Soup

1. Farley, John. *The London Art of Cookery.* 12th edition. (London: Scatherd and Letterman, 1811), 135.

2. Adams, Abigail. Letter to Mary Smith Cranch. 25 July 1784. [electronic edition] The Adams Papers Digital Edition, ed. C. James Taylor (Boston: Massachusetts Historical Society, 2007.) http://www.masshist.org/ff

Chapter 8: Puddings and Snacks

1. Adams, John. Letter to Abigail Smith, 13 April 1764 [electronic edition]. Adams Family Papers: An Electronic Archive. Massachusetts Historical Society. http://www.masshist.org/digitaladams/

2. Adams, Abigail. Letter from Abigail Adams to John Adams, 26 October 1799 [electronic edition]. Adams Family Papers: An Electronic Archive. Massachusetts Historical Society. http://www.masshist.org/digitaladams/

3 Adams, Abigail. Abigail Adams Diary of her Voyage from Boston to Deal, 20 June–20 July 1784: Thursday 24 June 1784. [electronic edition] The Adams Papers Digital Edition, ed. C. James Taylor. (Boston: Massachusetts Historical Society, 2007.) http://www.masshist.org/ff/

4. Adams, John. Letter to Louisa Catherine Adams, 1 January 1820, Adams Papers, 1639-1889, Microfilm edition, 608 reels (Boston: Massachusetts Historical Society, 1954-1959), reel #78, Massachusetts Historical Society.

5. Adams, John. Diary of John Adams, 23 August 1773. Wednesday. [electronic edition] Founding Families Digital Editions: Papers of the Winthrops and Adamses, (Boston: Massachusetts Historical Society.) http://www.masshist.org/ff (retrieved: 05/27/2012)

6. Adams, John. Diary of John Adams, 7 June 1771. [electronic edition] The Adams Papers Digital Edition, ed. C. James Taylor. (Boston: Massachusetts Historical Society, 2007.) http://www.masshist.org/ff/

7. Adams, Abigail. Letter to Catherine Nuth Johnson, 8 May 1801. Adams Papers microfilm: Reel 400. Massachusetts Historical Society.

8. Adams, Abigail. Letter to John Adams, 3 December 1788 [electronic edition]. Adams Family Papers: An Electronic Archive. Massachusetts Historical Society. http://www.masshist.org/digitaladams/

9. Adams, John. Diary of John Adams, 22 September 1774. [electronic edition] The Adams Papers Digital Edition, ed. C. James Taylor. (Boston: Massachusetts Historical Society, 2007.) http://www.masshist.org/ff/

10. Adams, John. John Adams diary 13, 1 March - 31 December 1766, March 1767 [electronic edition]. Adams Family Papers: An Electronic Archive. Massachusetts Historical Society.

Chapter 9: Dessert

1. Adams, John. Diary of John Adams, 8 September 1774. [electronic edition] The Adams Papers Digital Edition, ed. C. James Taylor. (Boston: Massachusetts Historical Society, 2007.) http://www.masshist.org/ff/

2. Adams, Abigail. Letter to Mary Smith Cranch. 6 October 1766. [electronic edition] The Adams Papers Digital Edition, ed. C. James Taylor. (Boston: Massachusetts Historical Society, 2007.) http://www.masshist.org/ff/

3. Adams, Abigail. Letter to Mary Smith Cranch. 24 [23] July 1778. [electronic edition] The Adams Papers Digital Edition, ed. C. James Taylor. (Boston: Massachusetts Historical Society, 2007.) http://www.masshist.org/ff

4. Adams, John. Diary of John Adams, 25. [i.e. 26] 1756. [electronic edition] The Adams Papers Digital Edition, ed. C. James Taylor. (Boston: Massachusetts Historical Society, 2007.) http://www.masshist.org/ff

5. Adams, John. Diary of John Adams, 10 April 1778. [electronic edition] The Adams Papers Digital Edition, ed. C. James Taylor (Boston: Massachusetts Historical Society, 2007.) http://www.masshist.org/ff

6. The Colonial Williamsburg Foundation. *Recipes from the Raleigh Tavern Bake Shop*. Virginia: The Colonial Williamsburg Foundation, 1991.), 3.

7. Lucy was the daughter of Mary Smith Cranch, who later married John Greenleaf.

8. Adams, Abigail. Abigail Adams to Lucy Cranch, 27 August 1785. [electronic edition] The Adams Papers Digital Edition, ed. C. James Taylor. (Boston: Massachusetts Historical Society, 2007.) http://www.masshist.org/ff

9. Briggs, Richard. *The English Art of Cookery*. (London, 1788.), 476.

Chapter 10: Drinks

1. Adams, John. Diary of John Adams, 26 July 1796. [electronic edition] The Adams Papers Digital Edition, ed. C. James Taylor. (Boston: Massachusetts Historical Society, 2007.) http://www.masshist.org/ff

2. Adams, John. Letter to Abigail Adams, 16 July 1777. [electronic edition] The Adams Papers Digital Edition, ed. C. James Taylor. (Boston: Massachusetts Historical Society, 2007.) http://www.masshist.org/ff

3. Adams, John. Diary of John Adams, 18 July 1796. [electronic edition] The Adams Papers Digital Edition, ed. C. James Taylor. (Boston: Massachusetts Historical Society, 2007.) http://www.masshist.org/ff

4. Wood, Gordon, ed. *John Adams: Revolutionary Writings, 1755-1775*. (New York: Library of America.), 324.

5. Adams, John. John Adams autobiography, part 2, "Travels, and Negotiations," 1777-1778. Part 2 is comprised of 37 sheets and 7 insertions; 164 pages total. Original manuscript from the Adams Family Papers, Massachusetts Historical Society.

6. Adams, John. Letter from John Adams to Abigail Adams, 22 February 1799. [electronic edition] The Adams Papers Digital Edition, ed. C. James Taylor. (Boston: Massachusetts Historical Society, 2007.) http://www.masshist.org/ff.

7. Hogan, Margaret A., C. James Taylor, Hobson Woodward, Hobson Woodward, Jessie May Rodrique, Gregg L. Lint, and Mary T. Claffey, eds. *Adams Family Correspondence*. (Cambridge: Harvard University Press, 2007), 8: 328-329.

8. Adams, John. Letter to Benjamin Rush, 3 September 1812. Adams Family Papers: Microfilm, Reel 118. (Boston: Massachusetts Historical Society)

9. Adams, Abigail. Letter to John Adams. 2 January 1779. [electronic edition] The Adams Papers Digital Edition, ed. C. James Taylor. (Boston: Massachusetts Historical Society, 2007.) http://www.masshist.org/ff/

10. Adams, John. Diary of John Adams, 17 December 1773. [electronic edition] The Adams Papers Digital Edition, ed. C. James Taylor. (Boston: Massachusetts Historical Society, 2007.) http://www.masshist.org/ff/

11. Graham, Judith S., Beth Luey, Margaret A. Hogan, C. James Taylor, eds. *Diary and Autobiographical Writings of Louisa Catherine Adams*. Volume I: 1778-1815. (Cambridge and London: The Belknap Press of Harvard University Press. 2013.), 179

12. Graham, Judith S., Beth Luey, Margaret A. Hogan, C. James Taylor, eds. Diary and Autobiographical Writings of Louisa Catherine Adams. Volume I: 1778-1815. (Cambridge and London: The Belknap Press of Harvard University Press. 2013.), 173.

13. Adams National Historical Park Guide Book, P.9

14. Adams, John. Letter from John Adams to Abigail Adams, 14 May 1777. [electronic edition] Adams Papers Digital Edition, ed. C. James Taylor. (Boston: Massachusetts Historical Society.) http://www.masshist.org/ff/

15. Mitchell, Stewart, Ed. *New Letters of Abigail Adams: 1788-1801.* (New York: Houghton & Mifflin C. 1947.), 107

16. Mitchell, Stewart, Ed. *New Letters of Abigail Adams: 1788-1801.*(New York: Houghton & Mifflin C. 1947), 106-7.

17. Adams, John. Letter from John Adams to Abigail Adams, 1 January 1799. [electronic edition]. Adams Family Papers: An Electronic Archive. Massachusetts Historical Society. http://www.masshist.org/digitaladams/

18. Adams, John. Diary 28, 6 February - 21 November 1777 [electronic edition]. Adams Family Papers: An Electronic Archive. Massachusetts Historical Society. http://www.masshist.org/digitaladams/

19. Vaille, F.O. and H.A. Clark. *The Harvard Book. A Series of Historical, Biographical, and Descriptive Sketches*, Vol. I. (Cambridge: Welch, Bigelow, and Company, University Press. 1875.), 29

20. Adams, John. John Adams diary, 15 August-3 September 1774 [electronic edition]. Adams Family Papers: An Electronic Archive. Massachusetts Historical Society. http://www.masshist.org/digitaladams

21. Adams, John. John Adams diary 21, 15 August-3 September 1774 [electronic edition]. Adams Family Papers: An Electronic Archive. Massachusetts Historical Society. http://www.masshist.org/digitaladams/

Chapter 11: Bills of Fare

1. Adams, Charles Francis, ed. *The Works of John Adams, Second President of the United States* (Boston: Little, Brown and Company, 1854.), 9: 92

2. Cappon, Lester J., ed. *The Adams-Jefferson Letters: The Complete Correspondence between Thomas Jefferson & Abigail & John Adams.* (Chapel Hill & London: The University of North Carolina Press.), xliv.

Epilogue

1. Adams, Abigail. Letter to John Adams, 7 April 1783 [electronic edition]. Adams Family Papers: An Electronic Archive. Massachusetts Historical Society. http://www.masshist.org/digitaladams/

2. Adams, John. Letter to Elias Boudinot. 18 Aug. 1801. John Adams Letterbook:"Public 7 Mar.- 20 June 1797; "Private" 23 Mar. 1801- 26 Nov. 1812. P-54, Reel 118 (Boston: Massachusetts Historical Society.)

Bibliography

The following list of books are some of the works that I used in writing this cookbook. They are a mix of primary and secondary sources. The majority of the cookbooks that I selected for my work were published during John and Abigail's lifetimes. Some of them were probably owned by the Adamses.

Unlike most of our nation's founding couples, John and Abigail left a rich collection of letters for future generations to learn about their lives. Advanced technology allows you to access most of their letters through the Massachusetts Historical Society's website, which is listed here as a source. Thanks in large part to David McCullough's best-selling biography of John Adams and the HBO's mini-series *John Adams*), numerous biographies of John and Abigail have been recently published. I recommend here a few of them that I found particularly helpful. The list of secondary sources includes valuable resources for learning about the time that the Adamses lived and selected biographies of the Adamses.

Robert Allison's short histories of the Boston Massacre and the Boston Tea Party help the reader get an overview of and insight into these historical events.

I selected a few contemporary published cookbooks as sources, such as Julia Child's, as they served me as general guides on cooking. I used these cookbooks during the process of testing the recipes in this book.

Photo by Ed Nute

Primary Sources

These primary sources include edited versions of John Adams's papers, letters of John and Abigail Adams, microfilm, and books published in John Adams's time.

The Adams Family Papers, 1639-1889. Microfilm edition, 608 reels. Boston: Massachusetts Historical Society, 1954-1959.

Adams, Charles Francis, Ed. *Familiar Letters of John Adams and His Wife Abigail Adams during the Revolution. With a Memoir of Mrs. Adams.* Boston: Houghton, Mifflin and Company. The Riverside Press, Cambridge. 1875.

Adams, Charles Francis. *Letters of Mrs. Adams, the Wife of John Adams. With an Introductory Memoir by her Grandson, Charles Francis Adams.* Vol. I. Second Edition. Boston: Charles C. Little and James Brown. 1840.

Adams, Charles Francis. *Letters of Mrs. Adams, the Wife of John Adams. With an Introductory Memoir by her Grandson, Charles Francis Adams.* Vol. II. Boston: Charles C. Little and James Brown. 1840.

Biddle, Alexander, ed. *Old Family Letters: Copied from the Originals for Alexander Biddle. Series A.* Philadelphia: Press of J. B. Lippincott Company. 1892.

Biddle, Alexander, ed. *Old Family Letters: Copied from the Originals for Alexander Biddle. Series B.* Philadelphia: Press of J. B. Lippincott Company. 1892.

Boswell, James. *Life of Johnson, in Two Volumes.* Vol. I, 1709-1776. London: Henry Frowde. 1904.

Cappon, Lester J., ed. *The Adams-Jefferson Letters: The Complete Correspondence Between Thomas Jefferson and Abigail and John Adams.* Charlotte: The University of North Carolina Press. 1988.

De Windt, Caroline Amelia Smith, ed. *Journal and Correspondence of Miss Adams, Daughter of John Adams, Second President of the United States.* Written in France and England, in 1785. Two Volumes. New York: Wiley and Putnam. 1841.

Diggins, Jack, ed. *The Portable John Adams.* New York: Penguin Classics. 2004.

Graham, Judith S., Beth Luey, Margaret A. Hogan, C James Taylor, eds. *Diary and autobiographical Writings of Louisa Catherine Adams.* Vol. i: 1778-1815. Cambridge and London: The Belknap Press of Harvard University Press, 2013.

Head, Richard. *The English Rogue: Continued in the Life of Meriton Latroon, and other Extravagants. Comprehending the Most Eminent Cheats of Most Trades and Professions.* London: Printed for Francis Kirkman. 1671.

Hogan, Margaret A., ed. and C. James Taylor. *Dearest Friends: Letters of John & Abigail Adams.* Cambridge: Belknap Press of Harvard University Press. 2007.

Johnson, Samuel. *The Works of Samuel Johnson, Vol. 9.* London: Printed for Bell & Bradfute, James M'Cleish, and William Blackwood. 1806.

Johnson, Samuel, William Shakespeare, George Steevens, Isaac Reed. *The Plays of William Shakespeare in ten volumes: with corrections and illustrations of various commentators,* Vol. II. London: Printed for C. Bathurst. 1778.

Kaminski, John P., ed. *The Quotable Abigail Adams.* Cambridge: Belknap Press of Harvard University Press. 2009.

Knapp, Samuel Lorenzo. *Biographical Sketches of Eminent Lawyers, Statesmen, and Men of Letters.* Boston: Richardson and Lord, 1821.

Lawson, John. *A New Voyage to Carolina: Containing the Exact Description and Natural History of that Country.* London. 1709.

Marquis de Chastellux, Francois Jean. *Travels in North America, in the Years 1780-81-82.* New York: White, Gallaher, & White, 7 Wall-Street. 1827.

Mitchell, Stewart, ed. *New Letters of Abigail Adams: 1788-1801.* Boston: Houghton Mifflin Company. 1947.

Peak, Jr., George A., ed. *The Political Writings of John Adams: Representative Selections* (The American Heritage Series). Indianapolis: Hackett Publishing Company, Inc. 2003.

Shuffelton, Frank, ed. *The Letters of John and Abigail Adams.* 4th Edition. New York: Penguin Classics. 2003.

Skinner, John S. ed. *American Farmer Containing Original Essays and Selections on Rural Economy and Internal Improvements.* Vol. IV. Baltimore: Printed by J. Robinson, Circulating Library. 1823.

Sylvanus Urban [Edward Cave] *The Gentleman's Magazine and Historical Chronicle*, Volume XL. For the Year MDCCLCC. London: Printed at St. John's Gate, for D. Henry. 1770

The Weekly Entertainer: or agreeable and instructive Repository Containing A Collection of Select Pieces Both in Prose and Verse; Curious Anecdotes, Instructive Tales, and Ingenious Essays on Different Subject. Vol. III, January 1784. Sherborne: Printed by R. Goadby and Co. 1784.

Wood, Gordon, ed. *John Adams: Revolutionary Writings, 1755-1775.* New York: The Library of America. 2011.

Cookbooks

These cookbooks were available in John Adams's time. Most can be found on Google eBooks or through archive.org. Several are part of the manuscript collection at the Massachusetts Historical Society.

W. M. (Anonymous). *The Compleat Cook: Expertly Prescribing the Most Ready Wayes, Whether Italian, Spanish, or French for Dressing of Flesh, and Fish: Ordering of Sauces, or Making of Pastrey.* London: printed by E. B. for Nath Brook, at the Angel in Cornhill, 1658.

Anonymous. *Cookery Reformed: Or, the Lady's Assistant.* London: Printed for P. Davey and B. Law, at the Bible and Ball in Avemary Lane, 1755.

Anonymous. *French Domestic Cookery, by an English Physician.* London: Printed for Thomas Boys, 7, Ludgate-Hill, 1825.

Anonymous. *The Lady's Companion: Or, An infallible guide to the fair sex.* The Fourth Edition, with large Additions. Vol. I. London: Printed for T. Read. 1743.

Anonymous. *Recipes book.* (Manuscript) Boston: Massachusetts Historical Society. Circa 1800.

Best, Michael R., Ed. Gervase Markham's *The English Housewife.* Montreal: McGill-Queen's University Press. 1986.

Bradley, Martha. *The British Housewife. or the Cook, Housekeeper's and Gardiner's Companion.* Vols. 2 and 3. London: Printed for S. Crowder and H. Woodgate. 1770 edition. Rockefeller Library, Colonial Williamsburg Foundation.

Briggs, Richard. *The English Art of Cookery.* London: G.G J. and J. Robinson. 1788.

Carter, Charles. *The Compleat City and Country Cook: or, Accomplish'd Housewife.* London: Printed for A. Bettesworth and C. Hitch; and C. Davis in Pater-noser Row: T. Green at Charing-Cross; and S. Austen in St. Paul's Church-yard. 1732.

Carter, Susannah. *The Frugal Housewife: Or, Complete Woman Cook.* Philadelphia: James Carey. 1796 edition. (Google eBook)

Child, Maria Lydia. *The American Frugal Housewife.* Twelfth Edition. Boston: Carter, Hendee, and Co. 1833. Reissued in 1989; Bedford: Applewood Books.

Cleland, Elizabeth. *A New and Easy Method of Cookery.* Edinburgh: Printed for the Author by W. Gordon, C. Wright, S. Willison and J. Bruce. 1755.

Collingwood, Francis & John Wollams. *The Universal Cook and City and Country Housekeeper.* London: Printed by R. Noble, for J. Scatcherd and J. Whitaker. 1792.

Dalgairns, Mrs. *The Practice of Cookery: Adapted to the Business of Every Day Life.* Third Edition. Edinburgh: Printed for Robert Cadell, Edinburgh: Simpkin and Marshall, London and all booksellers. 1830.

Eaton, Mary. *The Cook and Housekeeper's Complete and Universal Dictionary.* Bungay: Printed and Published by J. and R. Childs. 1823.

Edlin, Abraham. *A Treatise on the Art of Bread-making.* London: Printed by J. Wright, St. John's Square, for Vernor and Hood, Poultry. 1805.

Emerson, Lucy. *The New England Cookery, or The Art of Dressing All Kinds of Flesh, Fish, and Vegetables.* Montpelier: Printed for Josiah Parks. 1808. (www.archive.org)

Farley, John. *The London Art of Cookery.* 12th Edition. London: Scatcherd and Letterman. 1811.

Glasse, Hannah. *The Art of Cookery Made Plain and Easy, By a Lady.* London: 1784. (Google eBook)

Glasse, Hannah. *The Complete Confectioner; or, Housekeeper's Guide, By Mrs. H. Glass, Author of the Art of Cookery, with Considerable's Additions and Corrections, by Maria Wilson.* London: J.W. Myers and For West and Hughes. 1800.

Harrison, Sarah. *The House-Keeper's Pocket-Book, and Compleat Family Cook. By Mrs. Sarah Harrison, of Devonshire.* London: Printed for R. Ware. 1739.

Hayes, Thomas. *Concise Observations on the Nature of Our Common Food, Second Edition.* New York: Swordses for Berry & Rogers. 1790.

Johnstone, Christian Isobel. *The Cook and Housewife's Manual. By Mrs. Margaret Dods, of the Cleikum Inn, St. Ronan's.* Edinburgh: Printed for the Author. 1826.

Kitchiner, William. *Apicius Redivivus: Or, The Cook's Oracle.* The Fourth Edition. London: Printed for A. Constable & Company, Edinburgh, and Hurst, Robinson & Company, Cheapside. 1822.

MacIver, Susanna. *Cookery and Pastry, as taught and Pracitised by Mrs. MacIver, Teacher of those Arts in Edinburgh.* A New Edition, with Additions. London: Printed for C. Elliot and T. Kay. 1789.

Mason, Charlotte. *The Lady's Assistant for Regulating and Supplying her table, Being a Complete System of Cookery.* Third Edition. Printed for J. Walter, at Homer's Head, Charing-Cross. 1777.

May, Robert. *The Accomplisht Cook or, The Whole Art and Mystery of Cookery, fitted for all Degrees and Qualities.* London: Printed for Obadiah Blagrave at the Bear and Star in St. Pauls, Church-Yard. 1685. (Guttenberg.org eBook).

Menon and Jean-Bonaventure Rougnard. *La Science du maitre-d'hôtel cuisinier, avec des observations sur la connoissance et les propriétés des alimens.* Paris: chez les libraires associciés, 1789.

Nott, John. *The Cook's and Confectioner's Dictionary: or, the Accomplish'd Housewife's Companion.* London: Printed for C. Rivington, at the Bible and Crown, in St. Paul's Church-yard. 1723.

Nutt, Frederick. *The Complete Confectioner: Or, The Whole Art of Confectionary.* New York: Richard Scott. 1807 reprint. (Google eBook)

Nutt, Frederick. *The Imperial and Royal Cook: consisting of the Most Sumptuous made dishes, ragouts, fricassees, soups, gravies, &c.* London: Printed for Mathews and Leigh, Strand. 1809.

Parkinson, Richard. *Tour in America in 1798, 1799, and 1800: Exhibiting Sketches of Society and Manners, and A Particular Account of the American System of Agriculture, with its Recent Improvements, Volume 2.* Printed for J. Harding, St. James's Street; and J Murray, Fleet Street. 1805.

Perkins, John. *Every Woman Her Own House-Keeper; Or The Ladies' Library.* Fourth Edition, with Addition. London: Printed for James Ridgway. 1796.

Radcliffe, M. *A Modern System of Domestic cookery, or, The Housekeeper's Guide: Arranged on the Most Economical Plan for Private Families.* Manchester: Printed and Published by J. Gleave. 1823.

Raffald, Elizabeth. *The Experienced English Housekeeper, A New Edition.* Philadelphia: James Webster. 1818.

Rundell, Maria Eliza Ketelby. *American Domestic Cookery: Formed on Principles of Economy, for the Use of Private Families.* New York: Printed for Evert Duyckinck. 1823 edition.

Rundell, Maria Eliza Ketelby. *A New System of Domestic Cookery: formed upon principles of economy, and adapted to the use of private families throughout the United States.* By a Lady. New York: R. M'Dermut and D.D. Arden. 1814.

Simmons, Amelia. *The First American Cookbook, A Facsimile of "American Cookery" 1796.* With an Essay by Mary Tolford Wilson. New York: Dover Publications, Inc. 1984.

Simmons, Amelia. *American Cookery.* Facsimile of the 2nd ed., 1796. Introduction by Karen Hess. Bedford: Applewood Books. 1996.

Smith, Eliza. *The Compleat Housewife or Accomplish'd Gentlewoman's Companion.* London: Printed for J. and J. Pemberton. 1739 editon.

Smith, Robert. *Court Cookery, or the Compleat English Cook.* London: Printed for T. Wotton. 1725.

Tudor, William. *Miscellanies.* Boston: Wells and Lilly. 1821

Williams, T. *The Accomplished Housekeeper, and Universal Cook.* London: Printed for J. Scatcherd. 1797.

Woolley, Hannah. *The Compleat Servant-Maid: Or, The Young Maidens Tutor.* Printed for T. Passinger. 1677.

Secondary Sources

These include biographies of the Adamses and histories of significant events. Some of the following can easily be found on Google eBooks and archive.org.

Adams, Charles Francis and John Quincy Adams. *John Adams* (An American Statesmen Biography, Two-Volume Set, with an introduction by Peter Shaw). New York: Chelsea House Publishers. 1980.

Adams, Charles Francis, Ed. *Memoirs of John Quincy Adams: Comprising Portions of His Diary from 1795 to 1848*. Philadelphia: J. B. Lippincott & Co. 1877.

Adams, Charles Francis. *Three Episodes of Massachusetts History*. Boston & New York: Houghton Mifflin and Company. 1892.

Allison, Robert J., Ed. *American Eras: The Revolutionary Era, 1754-1783*. Detroit: Gale Research, 1998.

Allison, Robert J. *The American Revolution: A Concise History*. New York: Oxford University Press. 2011.

Allison, Robert J. *The Boston Massacre*. Beverly: Commonwealth Edition. 2006.

Allison, Robert J. *The Boston Tea Party*. Beverly: Commonwealth Edition. 2007.

Allison, Robert J. *The Crescent Obscured: The United States and the Muslim World, 1776-1815*. Chicago: University of Chicago Press. 2000.

Allison, Robert J. *A Short History of Boston*. Beverly: Commonwealth Editions. 2004.

Allison, Robert J. *A Short History of Cape Cod*. Beverly: Commonwealth Editions, 2010.

Barratt, Carrie Rebora and Paul Staiti. *John Singleton Copley in America*. New York: The Metropolitan Museum of Art. 1995.

Brookhiser, Richard. *America's First Dynasty: The Adamses, 1735-1918*. New York: The Free Press. 2002.

Candage, Rufus George Frederick. *Jeremy Gridley; Paper read Before the Society, October, 22. 1902*. Brookline: Brookline Society, 1903.

Clark, George Larkin. *Silas Deane, a Connecticut Leader in the American Revolution*. New York: G.P. Putnam's Sons, 1913.

Conroy, David W. *The Public Houses; Drink and the Revolution of Authority in Colonial Massachusetts*. Chapel Hill: University of North Carolina Press. 1995.

Davis, William Thomas. *History of the Judiciary of Massachusetts: including the Plymouth and Massachusetts colonies, the province of the Massachusetts Bay, and the Commonwealth*. Boston: Boston Book Company. 1900. (Google eBook)

Drowne, Henry Russell. *A Sketch of Frances Tavern and Those Connected with Its History*. New York: Frances Tavern, 1919.

Earle, Alice Morse. *Customs and Fashions in Old New England*. New York: Charles Scribner's Sons. 1893.

Ellis, Joseph J. *First Family: Abigail & John Adams*. New York: Alfred A. Knopf. 2010.

Ellis, Joseph J. *Founding Brothers: The Revolutionary Generation*. New York: Vintage Books, Random House, Inc. 2000.

Ellis, Joseph J. *Passionate Sage: The Character and Legacy of John Adams*. New York: W. W. Norton & Company. 1994.

Emerson, Ralph Waldo. *The Works of Ralph Waldo Emerson, Vol. III.: Society and Solitude, Letters and Social Aims, Addresses*. London: G. Bell & Sons. 1904. (Google eBook)

Ferling, John. *Adams vs. Jefferson: The Tumultous Revolution of 1800*. New York: Oxford University Press. 2004.

Frothingham, Richard. *History of the Siege of Boston, and of the Battles of Lexington, Concord, and Bunker Hill, Sixth Edition*. Boston: Little Brown and Company. 1903.

Holton, Woody. *Abigail Adams*. New York: Free Press. 2009.

Kaplan, Sidney and Emma Nogrady Kaplan. *The Black Presence in the Era of the American Revolution, Revised Edition*. Amherst: The University of Massachusetts Press. 1989.

Kiernan, Denise and Joseph D'Agnese. *Signing Their Lives Away: The Fame and Misfortune of the Men who signed the Declaration of Independence*. Philadelphia: Quirk Books. 2009.

Levin, Phyllis Lee. *Abigail Adams: a biography*. New York: St. Martin's Press, A Thomas Dunne Book. 1987.

Massachusetts. Office of the Secretary of the Commonwealth. *Massachusetts Soldiers and Sailors of the Revolutionary War: a compilation from the archives, prepared and published by the Secretary of the Commonwealth in accordance with chapter 100, resolves of 1891*. Boston: Wright & Potter Printing Co., State Printers. 1896-1908.

McCullough, David. *1776*. New York: Simon & Schuster. 2005.

McCullough, David. *John Adams*. New York: Simon & Schuster. 2001.

Morgan, Edmund S. *The Birth of the Republic: 1763-89. Third Edition*. Chicago: The University of Chicago Press.1992.

Nathan, Gavin R. *Historic Tavern of Boston*. New York: iUniverse. 2006.

Nigel, Paul C. *The Adams Women: Abigail and Louisa Adams, their sisters and daughters*. Cambridge: Harvard University Press.1999

Oliver, Sandra L. *Food in Colonial and Federal America*. Westport, Connecticut: Greenwood Press. 2005.

Richards, Laura Elizabeth Howe. *Abigail Adams and Her Times*. New York: D. Appleton and Company. 1917.

Savage, Neil J. *Extraordinary Tenure. Massachusetts and the Making of the Nation, from President to Speaker O'Neill*. Worcester: Ambassador Books, Inc. 2004.

Shepherd, Jack. *The Adams Chronicles: Four Generations of Greatness, introduction by Daniel J. Boorstin*. Boston: Little Brown & Company. 1985.

Smithsonian Institution. *The Smithsonian Institution: Documents relative to its origins and history*. 1879. (Google eBook).

Tyler, Mary Hunt Palmer. *Grandmother Tyler's book: the recollections of Mary Palmer Tyler (Mrs. Royall Tyler)/ edited by Frederick Tupper and Helen Brown Tyler*. New York: G. P. Putnam. 1925.

Tyler, Royall. *The Algerine Captive: Or the Life and Adventures of Doctor Updike Underhill, Six Years a prisoner among the Algerines. Two Volumes in One*. Hartford: Peter B. Gleason and Co. 1816.

Toll, Ian W. *Six Frigates: The Epic History of the Founding of the U.S. Navy*. New York: W.W. Norton & Company, 2008.

Vaille, F.O. and H.A. Clark. *The Harvard Book. A Series of Historical, Biographical, and Descriptive Sketches, Vol. I*. Cambridge: Welch, Bigelow, and Company, University Press. 1875. (Accessed by Massachusetts Historical Society.)

Vrabel, Jim. *When in Boston: A Time Lone & Almanac*. Boston: Northeastern University Press. 2004.

Withey, Lynne. *Dearest Friend: A Life of Abigail Adams*. New York: Simon & Schuster. 1981.

Wulf, Andrea. *Founding Gardeners: The Revolutionary Generation, Nature, and the Shaping of the American Nation*. New York: Alfred A. Knopf. 2012.

Cookbooks and references

These are contemporary works used for general cooking reference.

Child, Julia. *Mastering the Art of French Cooking.* New York: Alfred A. Knopf. 2009.

Child, Julia and Alex Prud'Homme. *My Life in France.* New York: Anchor Books. 2009.

Child, Julia. *The Way to Cook.* New York: Alfred A. Knopf. 1989.

Child, Lydia Maria. *The American Frugal Housewife. Dedicated to Those Who Are Not Ashamed of Economy.* 12th ed. Boston: Carter, Hendee, and Co. 1833.

Clark, Melissa. *The New York Times*, Dining Section. New York: The New York Times. 2011.

The Colonial Williamsburg Foundation. *Recipes from the Raleigh Tavern Bake Shop.* Virginia: The Colonial Williamsburg Foundation. 1991.

Davidson, Alan. *The Oxford Companion to Food.* New York: Oxford University Press, 1999.

Donovan, Mary, Amy Hatrak, Frances Mills, Elizabeth Shull. *The Thirteen Colonies Cookbook.* New York: Praeger Publishers, Inc. 1975.

Ingraham, Mercy. "A Scottish New Year's Celebration." *Early American Life Magazine.* December 2011. (PPS: 56-57, 72-74.)

Mitchell, Patricia B. *Revolutionary Recipes; Colonial, Food, Lore, & More.* Chatham, VA: Mitchells Publications. 2011.

Rombauer, Irma, Marion Rombauer, and Ethan Becker. *The Joy of Cooking; 75th Anniversary.* New York: Scribner. 2006

Staib, Walter. *The City Tavern Cook Book: Recipes from the Birthplace of American Cuisine.* Philadelphia: Running Press. 2009.

Index